C000278252

Big Norm
Looking after No.1

The Mark Crossley story

With Ray Yeomans

First published in July 2011

Copyright © Mark Crossley

Pictures courtesy of the Nottingham Post, the Welsh FA, Chesterfield FC, Picture Proud Ltd and Robert Wilson

All rights reserved. No part of this publication may be reproduced, stored in or introduced into a retrieval system, or transmitted in any form or by any means (electronic, mechanical, recording or otherwise), without the prior written permission of the copyright owner

Printed in Great Britain by Hickling & Squires Ltd, Unit 1, Engine Lane, Moorgreen Business Park, Moorgreen, Nottingham NG16 3QU.

Published by Mark Crossley

Dedication

I dedicate this book to my Mum and Dad, I owe them so much. Also to Lilli-Jade and Tommy and Emma and Alfie. And to Alan Hill and Brian Clough, who was like a second father to me and gave me my big break in football.

Acknowledgements

My thanks go to Dave Willans, Paul White, Mark Kelly and James Hallam

And to Ray Yeomans, at the Nottingham Post, who somehow managed to translate my random memories into the pages of this book.

I sincerely hope you enjoy reading it as much as I've enjoyed doing it...........

CONTENTS

Foreword

NORMALLY the popularity of someone in the dressing room can be gauged by the amount of nicknames they have. In Mark's case they varied from Norm, Ludo and Bosley to Roland and Zubi. Mind you, Brian Clough had a few others for him!

My earliest memories of Norm were when we were sitting in an hotel in Spain with the rest of the Forest squad when he declared: "I am the future!" Time has shown that he was, in the months and years to come. He had great ability, especially kicking away poor backpasses from me, but then he always did fancy himself as a striker.

Every Friday we used to practice penalties and Norm was the perfect goalkeeper to practice with, as his penalty-saving record in the FA Cup and his save from Matt LeTissier illustrate. We got on well and also shared a love of horse racing. Together with my wife, we owned a couple of horses over the years and we had some great days out at the Cheltenham Festival. It got a bit lively at times, to be fair. One year we had drunk a fair bit and Norm decided he wanted to buy a hat. He reached over to get a trilby, fell over and took the whole stand with him. He jumped straight back up, dusted himself off and said: "I don't think I'll bother after all." It was like a scene straight out of Only Fools and Horses.

Another thing I remember about Norm is his spotty backside. He had so many spots on his bum it looked as though someone had been using him as a dart board. You always knew when he was on the way to the shower after a game because the lads would shout "180."

It's no secret that Norm sometimes struggled with his weight. Every Friday when it was time to get on the scales he would try to lean on a table to try and take some of the weight off and he also developed the odd technique of leaning to one side, but it's good to see Norm embarking on a new career in coaching and I am sure that everyone who knows him wishes him well with that, because he is the future......

Former Forest & England star Stuart Pearce

I first met Crozz on a Welsh get-together for a game against the Republic of Ireland. I think we were both going to make our debuts. We met up at the training headquarters four days prior to the game. The first night we were sat in the bar and he looked all alone, so I invited him to sit with me and John Hartson. After the game the press dubbed us the Three Musketeers.

I soon realised that first night that he was one of us. We played pool that night and no-one else was allowed on the table. After that, we spent the next few days learning the national anthem. We had a right f...ing scream listening to Crozz trying to belt out the anthem in that Barnsley accent of his.

I once invited him down to my place for one of my shoots and, to be honest, he wasn't a bad shot with a twelve bore for a rookie. He brought his old man, Geoff, with him. He was one of the beaters and he went home with a dozen pheasants to flog on Barnsley market.

I have invited Crozz over to LA to stay with me. He is always welcome whenever he wants for as long as he wants, because he is a top man and I have a lot of time for him.

He was a top 'keeper and a great kicker and shot stopper. He was also ridiculously brave and thwarted my teams on many occasions. I am in the process of directing the remake of the film Escape to Victory and was thinking of offering him a part. But I need someone with the good looks and the ability of Sly Stallone in the original and I'm not convinced Crozz has that.........

Former Wales & Wimbledon star Vinnie Jones

I go back a long way with Mark. I was best man at his wedding and he was an usher at mine, but only because I had my brother as best man. Mark's a smashing lad and I don't know anyone who has a bad word to say about him. We hit it off like a house on fire and we did some crazy things when we were younger and didn't know any better.

One thing you can guarantee when Mark is around is that you'll have a few laughs. He has the knack of making people laugh without trying.

We've been through some good times and bad times together and he's always been there for me when I needed him. He's had his disappointments in life, but he's always bounced back from them. In the early days at Forest, when I came down from Preston, I used to give him a lift back home to Barnsley and pick him up from his parent's house. One morning I got there early and let myself in with the key. His mum and dad, who are the salt of the earth, thought they were being burgled, but it was just me making a cheeky cup of tea.

Eventually, we became neighbours in Aspley. He bought Steve Chettle's house, which backed onto mine. But Mark couldn't be bothered to walk round to my house so he just demolished the fence at the bottom of the garden instead. My mum used to come round on Saturday and leave me dinners for the rest of the week. I think Mark must have liked my mum's cooking, because he was always raiding the fridge at my place.

We liked to bet on pretty much anything when we were young and single. Once, four of us were playing golf at Ruddington and we decided whoever lost would pay for all the drinks that night. I was laughing going into the last hole because we were about ten shots up, but my partner ran into a bit of trouble and we ended up losing. After a few drinks Mark, and his partner, Stan Mitchell, decided it would be fun to have a couple of sips and then pour the rest onto the floor and order another one. He cost me a small fortune that night.

We had a lot of time on our hands in those days and we used to play snooker at Deverill's in Nottingham. One night we'd had about eight pints and decided to carry on drinking in town. We went to a club but Mark ended up throwing up all over the bar. Not his finest hour, but he's had plenty more to make up for it since then.

Former Forest striker Nigel Jemson

Fulham are in free fall. Three points away from the relegation zone, the media, if not screaming, suggesting that a recent intimation from boardroom level suggests management changes are to be considered. With fourteen goals having been conceded in the last four games, goalkeeper Tony Warner is attracting a lot of attention for the wrong reasons and the most influential player in the squad, team captain Luis Boa Morte, has had a less than inspirational spell in midfield. Morale is low and the media are aware of disputes between such people as Moritz Voltz and Zat Knight.

Young defender Liam Rosignior has leaked to the press that he would consider a move and, generally speaking, the future is looking far from rosy when the rumours run to a two game tolerance and the next game is Chelsea, a team sitting fifteen points clear at the top of the Premier and historically unbeaten by Fulham for 39 years.

I alerted Chris Coleman to the recognition that Mark Crossley is the best 'keeper at the club and had only ever been displaced through injury.But, quite apart from his goalkeeping abilities, he is an organiser and an influential presence, trusted by virtually every member of the team. Boa Morte is approached and agrees that, as a conscientious captain, his focus as a player is continually challenged and Norm agrees to act in a vice-captain's capacity, taking charge at the back, while Brian McBride brings his experience and professional bearing to the same role up front. Cookie and Keano have plotted, planned and developed the winning strategies throughout the season but, the singular difference now is that Boa Morte is freed up to be himself and the entire squad feel the energy and confidence to move forward in the knowledge that their final line of defence is everything that is possible. Not only is Crossley in goal, but the back four are also organised.

The result is an historic victory over Chelsea and a clean sheet with incredible performances from players such as Zat Knight and Mark Pembridge, a veteran who looked like he had shed ten years. Boa Morte scored the only goal and the critical mass that was Fulham, playing for each other, absorbed everything the highest paid team in Europe could throw at them.

The tactics were magnificent because Keano is magnificent in that department, the fitness was superb because it always had been at Fulham since the present management moved in, the squad was virtually the same and yet a team who had conceded fourteen goals and ended up squabbling amongst themselves had just reduced the Chelsea tidal wave to a squirt – and the difference was Mark Crossley and attitude.

'Practice is Physical – The Game is Emotional'
Motivational speaker Watt Nicoll

Introduction

Like Michael Palin, I suppose you could say I've gone full circle. I started off at Chesterfield as a kid and now I'm back at this great little club as reserve-team manager and goalkeeping coach. It's been an eventful journey, to say the least, via Nottingham Forest, Manchester United, Millwall, Sheffield Wednesday, Middlesbrough, Stoke, Fulham and Oldham.

I've got some great memories. I was at the birth of my three children and I wouldn't have missed that for the world. I actually cut the cord on my first son, Tommy. Unfortunately, I couldn't do it for Lilli because there were a few difficulties. But it was the best time in my life, seeing my children being born.

Because of football, I've seen a lot of the world, met some great people and also made a bob or two into the bargain. I've announced my retirement as a player now and just can't believe how the time has flown by.

I've had some right laughs along the way and plenty of heartache, not to mention backache. I've been at more cross-roads than a London cabbie. But, when I look back on my career, I think: "I didn't do too badly for a daft lad from Barnsley, did I?"

I don't have too many regrets, but one big one is obviously my failed first marriage. I love my kids and the bitter divorce hit me badly, not to mention costing me about a million quid!

Fortunately, I've never been a big spender, flash cars and that didn't interest me. I've never forgotten my roots in Barnsley and I have never lived beyond my means.

In football books you don't normally read much about what goes on behind the scenes; behind the locked doors in the dressing rooms.

But I tell it like it is in this book, I do not hold anything back....my brushes with the law, my broken marriage, my special relationship with Brian Clough, my clash with Pierre van Hooijdonk. The lot. It's all in here.

I once asked former Notts County goalkeeper Seamus McDonagh what time it was. He replied: "The time of your life. You are a professional footballer."

How right he was. I just wish some of the young kids these days felt the same way. All they care about is their mobile phones, massive head phones, Play Stations and their wages.

They rarely watch a football match and don't bother to find out anything about the opposition. They drive me mad with their egos, yet some of them can't even trap a ball.

They have Sunday and Wednesday off. They train at 10.30am and are finished by twelve, but they still have the cheek to turn up late. I can count on the fingers of one hand how many times I have been late in my career, but they drop in when they want.

While I was at Nottingham Forest, I was due to receive my Barclays Young Eagle on the Month award before a home game with Spurs. I used to give myself at least two hours to get to the ground to allow for traffic. This time I set off at 11am with my cousin Glenn and immediately ran into an accident.

The road was blocked and we did not move for about half an hour. When we finally got going again we ran into another traffic jam on the motorway. It left me with about half an hour to get to the ground.

My cousin told me to drive down the hard shoulder. It was risky, but I had no choice. It was panic stations, I can tell you. But we made it with about two minutes to spare.

The attitude of some young players frustrates me. It is always someone else's fault, never theirs. They earn so much that fines are not a deterrent any longer. It baffles me how some of them can be so unprofessional.

I wish I could make them see just how privileged they are, playing football and getting paid large sums of money to do it.

It is the best job in the world. I tell them to treasure it because your career can be ended by one bad tackle. Football has a nasty habit of kicking you in the balls. I should know that more than most. I tell them to make the most of every day and don't take it for granted, but it doesn't seem to sink in.

I'm a very placid man most of the time and I think I've started to develop good people skills over the years. But push me over the edge and I'll come down on you like a ton of bricks.

Alex Ferguson and Roy Keane had the right answer – zero tolerance, no matter how big a name they were dealing with.

Football changed me as a person – for the better I hope – and I've grown up a lot. I must admit that I've been a bit of a fool in the past and could have been more dedicated and professional at times. I spent too much time trying to please people and was too easily led.

I was a bit of a rogue when I was a lad and got into a few scraps. I liked a drink and a pretty girl, but who doesn't? It doesn't make me a bad person, does it?

I was just big, old, laid-back Norm. But, looking back, I was arrogant and immature at times. I did not realise how lucky I was and it wasn't until my Forest days in Europe that I grew up and started to plan for the future.

I'm a totally different person now. I'm certainly looking to the future now. I've got a new partner, Emma, a new baby, Alfie, and a five-year plan for my life. I know what I want to do and where I want to be.

I've passed all my coaching badges and I'd like to be a manager in my own right one day. I've played under something like twenty-one managers during my long career and I've learned something from all of them. I got my 'A' licence when I was at Fulham and I'm confident I can do the job, if and when the chance comes along.

Football is supposed to be a team game. But don't be fooled because it is really dog eat dog. It's every man for himself at the end of the day. The problem is that there is too much money in the game; too much jealousy. Top players simply have money to burn and they get bored.

That's why so many get into trouble. They are constantly in the public eye; under the microscope. They are an easy target when they go out on the town. A player gets into a little scuffle in a nightclub in the early hours of the morning and it's all over the national papers. Get involved with a girl, then it's all over five pages. I know!

I don't expect players to live the life of a recluse, but they have to be sensible. It's all wrong and it infuriates me.

So do football agents. Agents do your head in. Who invented them anyway? What do players need them for? Why can't they negotiate a wage rise for themselves? And why should they have to hand over a percentage of their earnings to a third party?

Look at the lad Bebe, who Manchester United signed for £7.4m. He was only twenty and had played just four pre-season matches for Vitoria Guimaraes when his new agent, who had only been with him for a few days, 'negotiated' the move to United.

The agent picked up 3.6m Euros for less than a week's work, the bulk of it for apparently selling the player's 'economic rights' to United. But Bebe, who was apparently homeless as a youngster, was allowed to go out on a season-long loan, with a view to a £2m transfer, after making just seven appearances. That's over £5m written off, just like that.

Some agents cause a lot of trouble and, maybe, the game would be better off without them.

Another problem is that managers are on a merry-go-round and some don't last five minutes before they fall off. The average life-span of a manager these days is less than two years.

You need a minimum of two years in the job, but lose five games in a row and you can be out of a job these days.

There were 40 sackings across the 92 League clubs last season, four more than the previous year. Just look at Craig

Short at Notts County and Roy Hodgson at Liverpool. They were not given enough time. Ronnie Moore got the chop at Rotherham after Chesterfield beat them 5-0.....and Rotherham were sixth in the League at the time!

And didn't Kevin Blackwell get the axe at Sheffield United just three games into the season? I also feel that all managers should have the right qualifications. It took me a year to get my 'B' licence and I had to pay £7,000 to get my pro licence.

It took me 18 months to get my Pro Licence. I used to fly over Belfast once a month after a game. Jim Magilton, Neil Lennon, Gerry Taggart and John Coleman were on the same course. I enjoyed every minute of it. It was brilliant. And I also made a lot of contacts, which is vital if you hope to go into management.

You need friends in the game because you never know when you might need a favour, or borrow a player for a month, things like that. Some people say it's a waste of time and money, but I disagree. I loved it. You are learning invaluable lessons from people who have been there and done that.

My first job in 'management' was in Nottingham when I helped manage a local Sunday League side, Sam Fays, along with my old mate Stan Mitchell.

I used to put up £10 for the man of the match out of my own pocket. It was the only way I could get the lads out of bed on a Sunday morning. It was a nightmare getting a team out some weeks. I also managed the Prospect Tavern, at Hoyland, when I was at Forest and I loved it.

We had a reunion at the pub recently and it was superb to meet up with lads I hadn't seen for 20 years. I used to take the job seriously because we had a good side and went right through the divisions. I really used to look forward to Sunday mornings. The fans used to vote for a man of the match every week and I'd buy the winner a pint as a reward. There was a family connection as well – my cousin was the goalkeeper!

Quite a few of the lads had been made redundant and couldn't find jobs in what was a working-class community and it brought home to me how lucky I was to be earning a good living as a professional footballer.

It is easy to lose touch when you are a professional footballer, but going back there every week took me back to my roots and put everything into perspective.

I like nothing better than going down the Queen's Head on Sunday. They've got ten televisions on the wall so you can watch any sport you want. I might move in there when I retire!

If I get a manager's job one day I don't want a contract. I want to be paid on results. I will say: "This is my points target for the first quarter of the season. Pay me a salary based on that. And the same for the second quarter and so on."

Maybe I will move back to London one day. And I would certainly love to go back to Forest in some capacity. I still love the club and always look for their result on a Saturday night. I once applied for a coaching job there, but the chief executive, Mark Arthur, told me to carry on getting my badges, which I did. They have my name on file. So you never know, maybe one day I might find myself back there.

The fact is, you never know what's around the corner in this game. I could have gone to Celtic as coach because I was on the same coaching course as Neil Lennon and got to know him.

Obviously Garry Parker, from my Forest days, was up there with him as well. It would have looked good on my CV, but I didn't fancy Scotland at the time, for various reasons, and didn't want to be pigeon-holed as just a goalkeeping coach.

I was keen to get into management, but I'm not so sure now because the pressures are huge, especially at the top of the tree. Carlo Ancelotti got the sack at Chelsea and they finished second in the Premiership!

I do some after-dinner speaking these days along with Darren Fletcher and John Styles and I really enjoy it. I used to crap myself at first because it is quite nerve-racking getting up there on your own.

But I think I'm getting better at it, especially after few drinks! I like to tell stories that I think are funny and make people laugh. They seem to like my impersonations of Brian Clough and Frank Clark. I'm currently working on an impression of John Sheridan, my manager at Chesterfield. I am happy learning off him. I think he will go far in the game, so I am trying to get it right. Just in case....

I worked hard to get my coaching certificates

Chapter One
I should have done better

I was born on June 16, 1969, in Sheffield. I had a brilliant upbringing in a local mining village. My dad was a miner before he retired and started up as a market trader at Chapeltown and Hoyland. My mum worked on the stall on Tuesday, Friday and Saturday so, for the majority of the time, I stayed with my grandparents, Elsie and James, and knocked about with my two cousins, Andy and Glenn.

My parents are absolutely brilliant, the salt of the earth. My dad played pool for South Yorkshire and also played football, until he broke his leg. They brought me up well and I was taught to be polite, respect the elderly and never look down my nose at anyone. My dad doesn't drink, so I don't know where I get my bad habits from! I swore at my dad once and he gave me a belt, so I never did that again....

I never really thought I'd be a footballer. I always thought I would follow them on to the markets and I still go down there on Saturday mornings, when I can, to chat to the customers.

I went to Hoyland Common Infants School, which has been knocked down now. When I was six I moved to the Juniors which was just a few yards from where we lived. It meant that I could stay in bed until a quarter to nine every morning and still not be late for class, which was great.

It was there I started playing football. Believe it or not, I was a regular goal-scorer with my head, going up for corners, and I also took penalties. It's true.

We had a good little side in those days. One week we won 32-0 and we topped the U-12 B division in 1980-81 with 21 wins out of 22, drawing the other game, scoring 183 goals and conceding only 14. I was captain at the time but I had the captaincy taken off me after chasing half the length of the pitch to 'strangle' a lad called Lee Burgin when he scored an own goal in the semi-finals of the All-schools. The final was at Oakwell and I hit the bar from the half-way line. I was ten at the time! We won, but I never had the honour of lifting the cup.

In those days the teacher had trouble getting us to away matches, so my dad used to take us in the back of his van, which was actually an old ambulance he had converted.

I wasn't a bad player. I couldn't run very fast, but passing was my strong point. Even at 15, I was tall for my age and maybe that helped me stand out. I was also good at cricket. I kept wicket for Hoyland St Peter's Cricket Club and was a good opening bat. I played in the Yorkshire League, alongside men, when I was 14 and I once hit 26 off one over in a charity game and then had to retire. Even when I was playing at Nottingham Forest, I carried on playing cricket for a local club called Edwalton, near Nottingham.

In one game we were up against former Forest favourite Bryn Gunn and I hit the third ball straight back over his head for six. I knocked him all over the ground. I got goalkeeper Dave Beasant to play for us once and he took a brilliant catch on the boundary.

I also played indoors at Basford, in Nottingham. They had a bowling machine there which the owner let us use. I took Nigel Jemson down to the nets one day and set the machine for 90 miles an hour, FULL TOSS. It missed his head by a fraction. Not one of my better ideas. I never stopped to think what would have happened if it had hit him in the mouth. At least it might have shut him up for five minutes!

I love the game and it was a toss-up at one stage which sport I picked, football or cricket. On one occasion I was playing in a final against Denaby when I hit the final ball for six. It won us the game and took me to 102.

I was also pretty good at basketball when I was at Hoyland

Kirk Balk School. The ball was bigger, so I didn't drop it so much! I liked any ball games – apart from rugby, it was too tough for me!

I liked school but, looking back, I should have done better (as you can see from my school reports, too easily distracted; chats too much, you get the idea). Perhaps they should chisel that on my tombstone. One teacher said I would never make anything of myself and that I'd end up on the dole. These days they have a picture of me and a signed shirt on the wall at the school.

I wasn't a bad lad, but I was easily distracted. The teachers at Junior school all liked me and one teacher, Ronnie Hallam, spent a lot of time working on improving my batting. The same lads played for the cricket and football team and everybody looked up to you. As a result we rarely got picked on although I still got into scraps.

It was different when I got to Senior school. One teacher, Mrs Manion, didn't like boys. She taught domestic science in our form room. One morning she had prepared a bowl of icing for her first lesson and every time I walked by I dipped my finger in. When she came in she noticed it had been tampered with.

She said: "Mark Crossley have you been at the icing?"

"No Miss, not me, honest Miss."

She said: "Mark Crossley go and look in the mirror." When I looked I had icing sugar all over my face. No wonder the rest of the class were laughing. But I wasn't laughing when she sent me to the headmaster, Roy Hilton, for a taste of the cane.

In 1979, I was in the Barnsley Boys side that won the Rocking Trophy U-13 five-a-side title. We had Gary Dewhurst in goal, Mark Kelly, Terry Fieldsend, Steven Berry and Mark Chapman. That season Hoyland Falcons won the Sheffield & District U-13 title. And we did it in style, thumping Hackenthorpe 6-0.

I never thought that I was going to be a goalkeeper in those days, in fact I didn't even end up playing in goal until I was 14, when Paul Heald, who had spells with Sheffield United, Orient and Wimbledon, where he was the back-up to former Forest 'keeper Hans Segers, was taken ill. I was selected for Barnsley Boys, but we lost 4-0 at home to Huddersfield in the 3rd round of the ESFA Gillette Trophy, under lights at Oakwell. I was gutted. The rest of the team was Andrew Skelton, Lee Parkinson, Peter Houghton, Shaun Haber, Mark Kelly (capt), Adam Pemberton, Glynn Pearson (Swales), Mark Johnson, Ian Wood (Levitt) and Hinchcliffe. I often wonder what happened to the rest of those lads.

I played for Bansley against Rotherham in the U-12 Cup final at Barnsley and went on a two-day trip to Belgium. We went into a big hall to be allocated the families we were staying with. When my name was called out a drunken bloke lurched towards me. I turned to my dad, crying and said: "I not staying with him." Fortunately, I was allocated another family and they were great.

As lads we played on a local field, just in the middle of a load of council houses really. It used to be like a scene out of the football match in the film 'Kes'. It's gone now. There is a nursing home where it used to be.

One day I remember coming home and a load of lads had got together and decided to form our own team. We all asked our parents if anyone was interested in running it and my dad volunteered. He was involved with the club for thirteen years and when he packed in they had grown to seven teams and had £7,000 in the bank.

Sundays from then on were based around Sunday league football with Hoyland Common Falcons U-11's, training twice a week, on Tuesday and Thursday nights. It was absolutely brilliant and the local community loved it. My uncle, Alan Crossley, was involved with the club which also produced Chris Morgan, who did so well with Sheffield United.

The club was well run, it is almost like an academy, and is

still going strong to this day. I look forward to going back to help present the awards every year. When I was 15, I eventually graduated to Hoyland Town Jaguars, who were the top men's team locally and produced Billy Whitehurst, who played for about ten League clubs, and John Schofield (Barnsley). We won everything the Sheffield & District League had to offer and got to the area final at Bramall Lane.

I missed the semi-final because I was on holiday but the manager, Sam Pickering, brought me back for the final, which was watched by loads of scouts. If it wasn't for him, I suppose I wouldn't be where I am today.

I used to work Saturdays, for pocket money, £5, I think. I also used to skip school a lot in my final year, as you can see from my report card. I was crafty and would only bunk off when I knew my mum and dad were out working.

I used to support Leeds, along with my dad, as a kid. Alan Clarke was my favourite. I think I was seven or eight when my dad took me to Elland Road for the first time, to see them play QPR. They had a great side in those days with Harvey, Reaney, Bremner, Cherry, McQueen, Yorath, Hunter, Jordan and the two Grays.

I never thought about following in their footsteps. Then, one day, Paul Heald, pulled out and I went in goal....the rest, as they say, is history. We pipped Sheffield Wednesday Juniors 2-1 and the next week we beat Sheffield United 4-0.

One of their managers asked my dad if I was a ringer because I had played so well. When the regular 'keeper was fit again my dad wanted to put him back in for the cup final. But Graham Rooker, who ran the side with him, said he would quit the club if I was dropped. In the end my dad compromised and said we could play one half each. We won 6-1.

At 6ft 4 inch I suppose I was built for the role and it just seemed to come naturally after that. But I never had any proper goalkeeping coaching or training in those early days.

It all happened pretty quickly after that. Sheffield United, Sheffield Wednesday and Barnsley were all interested after watching us in the cup final and I was really keen to play for my home-town club. I played in goal for Barnsley reserves in a trial game but twisted my knee. Ronnie Glavin sent me to see the physio, Norman Rimmington, a great bloke who was still connected with the club well into his 80's. I sat around for ages and no-one came. In the end I took myself off to hospital and my dad came and picked me up. Next day my dad went down to the club and gave Ronnie a bollocking and that was the end of that.

Then a Chesterfield scout asked two or three of us to go to Saltergate for training and I got a game with their reserves, along with big Ernie Moss, when I was only 15. We played Ilkeston Town and won 2-1. I was very nervous, but the defence kept talking to me and encouraging me and, once I had a few touches of the ball, I soon settled down. The other game was against Shepshed, I think.

I'd never really thought much about being a professional footballer at that stage. I never had the appetite for it. But suddenly the penny dropped. If these clubs were interested in me, then perhaps I might be a decent player after all.

One day, my dad was approached by a Watford scout at a game. "Did I fancy going for a trial?" Why not. But would I want to live in Watford? Probably not. My dad was the driving force really. He said I would be stupid to waste the opportunity and he made me go.

Anyway, I thought I would give it a try. I was in digs with Dean and Dave Holdsworth, who both went into management with Newport and Mansfield Town. Future England 'keeper David James was just starting out on the road to stardom. It was OK, but we were staying with an elderly couple and I was sleeping on a camp bed.

I wasn't happy and couldn't wait to get back home to my mum's cooking, but Steve Harrison and Tom Waley persuaded me to go back for a second week and I played against Arsenal in a four-team tournament. Watford wanted to offer me YTS forms, but I got homesick again. I was so desperate I kept hitting my knee with a wet towel until it swelled up. Graham Taylor was the Watford manager at the time and I told him I wasn't happy. In fact, it was making me ill. Anyway, I caught the train home and never went back.

I can certainly sympathize with young players today. I can understand why they get depressed, especially if they are thrown on the scrapheap after a couple of years at a club, all their hopes and aspirations dashed.

Like them, I didn't know what the future held. By now I'd decided that I didn't really want to follow my dad onto the market, so I enrolled on a design course at college. It was just something to do, because I was bored stiff. But, when I got there I soon realised that it was really just a painting and decorating course.

I was working as well, as a part-time painter and decorator with my cousin, Mick Rodney, as well as doing the markets on Saturdays. I was bringing in a decent wage then, for a 17-year-old lad. I was only on £27.50 on a YTS and here I was raking in about £90 a week. I must have seemed like a millionaire to my mates. Obviously, being young and naive, it didn't really sink in that I really wanted to be a footballer. I was just bothered about money, I suppose.

Then, out of the blue, we got a call from a chap called Mick Raynor asking if I fancied having a trial with Forest Colts. Apparently, Jack Noble, the area scout for Forest, had recommended me, Mark Kingstone and Carl Butler. We were supposed to play three 20-minute games. After the first game, Alan Hill went to my dad and said Forest wanted to sign me.

I wasn't sure at the time because of the experience I'd had at Watford. But Brian Clough rang my dad and I ended up playing for the Colts. They wanted Mark Kingstone back as well, but he wouldn't go. He was a really good centre-half, but he just ended up playing amateur football. Some days I didn't feel like travelling to Nottingham, but my dad pushed me. He used to bribe me to go. He even bought me my first car, for £150, but I'd only had it a couple of days when I drove it into a wall trying to avoid some road works.

When my dad didn't drive me down to Forest, I had to catch a bus from Hoyland to Barnsley and then another to Sheffield to travel down to Nottingham. I'd then walk from the Victoria Centre bus station to the ground.

It was silly really because, when I got there, I used to really enjoy it. We had some good players too, like Wayne Manners who played in defence then, but went on to be a good striker in local football in the Nottingham area.

I even scored a goal for the Colts with a kick out of my hands. In another game, I was getting some right stick off their centre-half, who kept treading on my toes at corners. So, when one came across, I punched the ball away with one hand and his head with the other.

One day Brian Clough and Ron Fenton were at the ground and the boss said: "If you want to come and play for me, get your hair cut." Needless to say, his word was law in those days. I got a short-back-and-sides and stayed for the next 13 years ....

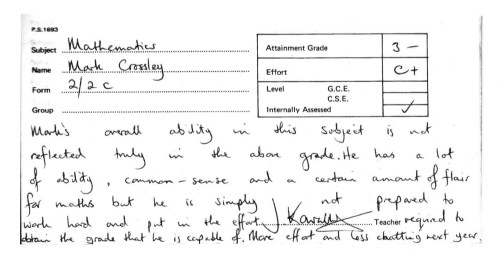

P.S.1693		
Subject English	Attainment Grade	2 −
Name CROSSLEY Mark	Effort	B
Form 2/2C	Level G.C.E. C.S.E.	
Group	Internally Assessed	✓

Mark has produced some pleasing work in English this year. He is an intelligent boy with a good sense of humour, which makes him an asset to oral work in class.

Technically there is room for improvement, particularly in the areas of paragraphing and punctuation. I hope that he will strive to concentrate on these problems, because he *H J Bell* will do even has some good ideas to express. My .... Teacher better! advice to Mark is to avoid letting himself be distracted by others – then he

Intelligent boy? Were they talking about me?

P.S.1693		
Subject Mathematics	Attainment Grade	3 −
Name Mark Crossley	Effort	C +
Form 2/2 C	Level G.C.E. C.S.E.	
Group	Internally Assessed	✓

Mark's overall ability in this subject is not reflected truly in the above grade. He has a lot of ability, common-sense and a certain amount of flair for maths but he is simply not prepared to work hard and put in the effort. *K avellt* Teacher required to obtain the grade that he is capable of. More effort and less chatting next year.

Not prepared to work hard! Sounds familiar....

P.S.1693

Subject	German	Attainment Grade	3
Name	Mark Crossley	Effort	6
Form	22c	Level G.C.E. / C.S.E.	
Group		Internally Assessed	✓

Mark has the ability to do quite well in this subject, if he wants to. Unfortunately, although he works quite well most of the time, he also has a tendency to mess around, when someone else is speaking.

.... M.Squire .... Teacher

Has the tendancy to mess around......

Scaled Mark 31

P.S.1693

Subject	History	Attainment Grade	4
Name	Mark Crossley	Effort	B|C
Form	2/2c	Level G.C.E. / C.S.E.	
Group		Internally Assessed	✓

Very disappointing, the has the ability to do much better than this. He must realise that to gain the full benefit of his education he must be willing to put in the effort all year round. He will only get one chance and I suggest he makes the most of it.

.... T.S.Bruce .... Teacher

Has the ability to do much better......

24

P.S.1693

Subject ..... GEOGRAPHY .....

Name ..... MARK CROSSLEY .....

Form ..... 2'2C .....

Group .....

Attainment Grade	3
Effort	C
Level G.C.E. C.S.E.	
Internally Assessed	✓

Mark has not tried hard enough in this subject. He has not concentrated sufficiently well on the lessons, or on the work that has been set. Mark will have to make more effort before any appreciable progress is made.

A Brocklehurst ..... Teacher

Not tried hard enough…..

P.S.1693

Subject ..... Religious Studies .....

Name ..... Mark Crossley .....

Form ..... 2 2 C .....

Group .....

Attainment Grade	3
Effort	C+
Level G.C.E. C.S.E.	
Internally Assessed	.

When Mark settles down he can produce some good work. There are occasions, however, when his concentration lapses and as a result his work suffers.

K. Richards ..... Teacher

Has lapses in concentration....

25

Subject ...... Integrated Science ......

Name ...... Mark Crossley ......

Form ...... 2/2C ......

Group ......

Attainment Grade		3 –
Effort		B
Level	G.C.E. C.S.E.	
Internally Assessed		

Mark's greatest problem is that he is inconsistent. In one lesson he can be wholly enthusiastic and produce some extremely good work. Yet on other occasions, he is lazy, careless, talkative and at times cheeky. His assessment tests have shown potential, but his exam result has badly let him down. His homework also needs improvement, both in _____ Osgood _____ Teacher presentation and in giving it in at the proper time.

Too inconsistent....

Subject ...... Woodwork ......

Name ...... Mark Crossley ......

Form ...... 2/2C ......

Group ......

Attainment Grade		2
Effort		B
Level	G.C.E. C.S.E.	
Internally Assessed		

Mark has done reasonably well in this subject, but is capable of doing better if he took more care and was more precise in following instructions. D. Goodwin _____ Teacher

Done reasonably well....

P.S.1693

Subject ...... *Metalwork* ......

Name ...... *Mark Crossley* ......

Form ...... *2/2K* ......

Group ......

Attainment Grade	2/3 -
Effort	B.
Level G.C.E.	
C.S.E.	
Internally Assessed	

Mark has maintained a steady consistent effort.
His work would improve with Just a little more care with
the finish

...... *Peter D Morris* ...... : Teacher

Consistent effort....

P.S.1693

Subject ...... *Housecraft* ......

Name ...... *Mark Crossley* ......

Form ...... *2c* ......

Group ......

Attainment Grade	5
Effort	B
Level G.C.E.	
C.S.E.	
Internally Assessed	

Mark does not work to the best of his
ability, his chief aim is to distrupt
and be the centre of attraction. Much
more effort is required on his part.

...... A Lockwood ...... Teacher

More effort required....

27

P.S.1693

Subject	Craft (Fabrics)	
Name	Mark Crossley	
Form	2/2c	
Group		

Attainment Grade		3
Effort		A.
Level	G.C.E.	
	C.S.E.	
Internally Assessed		

Mark always tries hard. He tends to want to do easy tasks without extending himself but he works well and is making pleasing progress

C. M. Benson. Teacher

Making pleasing progress....

P.S.1693

Subject	Art	
Name	MARK CROSSLEY	
Form	2/2c	
Group		

Attainment Grade		2
Effort		A
Level	G.C.E.	
	C.S.E.	
Internally Assessed		.

Mark can always be relied upon to produce a good standard of art work. I am pleased with his progress during the year.

Mr R.H. Teacher

A good standard. What me?

	Attainment Grade	
Subject _Physical Education_		
Name _Mark Crossley_	Effort	A-
Form _2/2C_	Level G.C.E.	
Group	C.S.E.	
	Internally Assessed	

Mark is a very keen member of the group, always trying his best, particularly in soccer. One slight fault with him is that he can sometimes become so involved that a decision or result against him can cause a little ill-feeling. He must make sure _____: Teacher that this does not develop.

A keen member of the group....

GENERAL REPORT

This is a report indicating the student's academic progress, conduct, and any special aptitudes or interest shown.

Name _Mark Crossley_   Number of:-

Form _22C_   Half days absent [16]   Times late [23] ✴

I do hope that Mark will take serious note of the comments made and I am sure that with a determined effort his next report will reflect his capabilities. He is a lively boy, sometimes a bit cheeky! and he participates willingly in form activities. _F. Richardson_ Form Tutor

Mark is hard working in some subjects and idle in others. This approach _D. Good_ Year Tutor will reduce his chances _Roy M⁻_ Head/Deputy
P.S.1694 of success at school.

A bit cheeky! What me?

29

That's me, aged 12, on my first day at senior school

A page boy at a wedding

My first holiday in the arms of my brilliant dad, Geoff

Me with my Grandmother Elsie

I settle in at Hoyland Common Infants School

Hoyland Common Falcons U-12's, the start of it all in 1981

Hoyland Juniors presentation in 1981. That's me with Glynn Pearson, Mark Kelly, Ian Wood and Steve Berry

The Hoyland Falcons team that lost in the U-13 KO Cup final

On the ball as captain of the Kirk-Balk School basketball team

Hoyland Common Junior School in 1978. Our teacher and manager, Paul Sylvester, was a superb bloke

The Barnsley Schools U-12 team that went to Belgium

The Birdwell Rovers Saturday team, which was run by Dave Copley

Me with the Hoyland Town Jaguars men's team

I'm pictured on the back row, along with Duncan Clay, Richard Nuttal, Steve Hopkinson, Dave Bond, Steve Troake, Paul Sylvester, Ashley Errat, Sam Pickering, Pete Kay and Neil Evans

The treasured picture of Brian Clough above my bed

CHAPTER TWO
The best manager in the world

I've got a painting of Brian Clough OBE hanging above my bed.
I like to think Old Big Head is still looking over me. It was a
Christmas present from my wife to be, Emma, because she said I
never stopped talking about him. I still don't. And I make no
apologies for that. That man was like a second father to me.

I was a bit of a rogue in my younger days and I think the
gaffer liked that. I was scared of him, he ruled by fear, but I was
also in awe of him. He once said that if I didn't make it as a
footballer I could get a job as a pit prop. And he joked that if you
put a crossbar and two goalposts side by side they still wouldn't
be as thick as me! He was probably right.

I used to avoid him if I saw him in a corridor at the City
Ground. Then I got wise. Instead of hiding I would walk straight
past him and say: "Morning gaffer, lovely day, would you like
a cup of tea or coffee?" It must have worked because, years later,
he came to my testimonial. But he didn't turn out for Des Walker
or Steve Chettle, did he?

Every man and his dog seem to have a story about Brian
Clough since his death. But have you heard the one about the
day he tried to hang me on a peg in the dressing room? It
happened after a game with Aston Villa when I saved a penalty
from my mate David Platt, of all people.

It was a dubious penalty, but fortunately the game finished
1-1. The gaffer, for some reason, was in a rage about it, even
though I saved it. After the match I waited to shake hands with
my opposite number, Nigel Spink I think, when the referee came
over and shook hands with me.

Suddenly the gaffer gave me a dig in the ribs from behind.
When I got back to the dressing room I started to take my jersey

off and had it above my head when he suddenly punched me in the stomach and tried to hang me on a peg. He was getting right stuck in, I can tell you, and Stuart Pearce had to jump in to rescue me. "If you shake hands with a ref again I'll chop your balls off," fumed Cloughie. No "Well done Barnsley" for saving a penalty and earning us a point. Something had triggered his fit of temper but, to this day, I don't know what it was.

I wasn't the only one to get thumped in the stomach of course. When we reported back for pre-season Ron Fenton would punch us, hard, to make sure we weren't carrying any excess fat. And it came bloody keen, I can tell you. He came close to getting punched back a couple of times, but I suppose he was just following orders.

But the worst one was my best mate at Forest, Nigel Jemson. His crime? He had come on as substitute in a reserve game and committed the cardinal sin of putting a cross out of play and behind the goal. Cloughie confronted him in the dressing room and said: "Stand up. Is your mother here? I hope not because she would be ashamed of you." Then he said: "Have you ever been punched before?" And, with that he punched Jemmo really hard in the stomach. It was hard enough to knock the wind out of him and he was almost sick.

The national newspapers were on it like a shot the next day and reporters tracked us down to Mackay's cafe, where we used to meet up for coffee. But Jemmo, bless him, denied anything had happened. Wise move. He probably didn't want to risk getting thumped again!

My favourite Brian Clough story involves my old Wales team-mate Vinnie Jones and the Crazy Gang before a match with Wimbledon when Brian Clough was giving his team talk. The ball was in the middle of the dressing room on a towel and the gaffer went into his "God gave us grass to play on" speech. He didn't do it every home game, but he just liked to do it every now and again to remind us to keep the ball on the floor and pass it. Just then we heard this loud noise coming from the opposing dressing room. "Alan Hill, go and see what's making that fucking noise," barked Clough. "It's the away team, they've got a ghetto blaster boss," replied Hill. "Fucking ghetto blaster, what the hell is that? Go and ask them to turn it down," said Clough.

So Hilly went down the corridor, knocked on the door and asked a half-naked Vinnie Jones (not a pretty sight!) if he wouldn't mind turning the volume down a bit. "No problem," said Vinnie. But as soon as Hilly got back to the Forest dressing room, the Wimbledon lads cranked the noise up even louder.

"Go back again and ask them to turn the volume down...and this time, say please," said Cloughie.

So off went Hilly again. Again Vinnie came to door. "Turn the sound down, please," said Hilly. "Sure no problem squire," said Vinnie. Just as Hilly got back to the dressing room they turned up the decibels again. The gaffer could stand it no longer. He knocked on the door, brushed past Vinnie and, to the astonishment of the Wimbledon lads, picked the ghetto blaster up and smashed it on the floor.

He said: "Now try and play your fucking music" and left. The Wimbledon lads were all stunned to put it mildly. We won 4-1.

You could always expect the boss to do the unexpected. Like the day he pulled Tommy Gaynor off the pitch for losing the ball. "I've not signed you to flick the ball, I've signed you to hold it," said the gaffer as Tommy was subbed.

We never got a team talk from the gaffer, he didn't really bother about the opposition. Often he'd sit in the dressing room throwing a cricket ball about or a squash ball. Sometimes he would skim his flat cap across the room and try and land it on a peg and Steve Chettle would have to pass it back to him. The referee would be banging on the door, but the boss would ignore him until he managed to land his cap on the peg. Only then could we go out and play.

Training with Brian Clough was also unusual. I shudder to

think what all today's fitness coaches and sports science gurus would make of his methods. We'd play five-a-side for a bit; some days we'd just go for a walk along the banks of the Trent. On other occasions the gaffer would suddenly turn up and say: "Run to that tree over there and get back in 60 seconds. That was 62 seconds, do it again." That was your warm-up.

And I wish I had £1 for every time I've missed training to take his dog for a walk. And then there was his garden, his pride and joy. He used to arrange for six of us to be picked up in the club mini-bus and taken to his home near Derby. There we would tidy up, rake up the leaves and burn them at the bottom of the garden. Our reward was a drink of wine in a plastic glass, dinner and a £5 note, taped to a box of chocolates, to take home. We had a rota and if your name was on it, you had to go. But I didn't mind really because you missed training and Mrs Clough, Barbara, made a fuss of us. She was a proper lady.

Brian Clough put me on the spot one day when I was playing in a reserve game against Huddersfield and I broke my finger. When I came off at half-time I started to take my boots off and told the gaffer that there was no way I could carry on. "Could you carry on for me Mark Crossley?" he asked. I could see Archie Gemmill nodding behind him. So what could I say? I carried on, with my fingers strapped together. I was having to save shots one-handed and I think I even headed a couple away! Needless to say, we lost, 5-1. After the game, the gaffer put his arm around me and gave me a kiss. Just then, my dad came over to see if I was OK and the boss told him to piss off and mind his own business.

On the coach afterwards he asked who the man was and I told him it was my father. The next day he sent chocolates, flowers and magazines to my folks by way of an apology.

After a game with Coventry, which we won 3-2, Cloughie asked me where I was going. I said I was going home to see my mum and dad. He had other ideas."No you are not; 9 o'clock my house tomorrow; bring your gloves and your boots." I hadn't got a clue what was going on. Come to think of it I had no idea how to get to his house then. Fortunately the groundsman knew the way and I duly turned up at the gaffer's front door. Mrs Clough opened the door and Brian shouted: "Thank you for agreeing to play for Simon's team, AC Hunters, today."

Suddenly the penny finally dropped. I went out to play for his son's Sunday side on a parks pitch in Derby. We won 4-0, but I think they later had the points deducted. Cloughie was on the touchline with his dog and every time I got the ball I could hear him shouting "Barnsley". Maybe it was his way of bringing me back down to earth.

Signing my first decent contract with Forest was absolutely amazing. I got a telephone call to come in and see the gaffer. As it happens, he'd been in the bath and shouted for me to get him a towel. I tracked his wet footprints to the sauna and he told me to come and see him on Monday morning, there'd be a new contract waiting for me, which was totally unexpected.

Come Monday morning, I knocked on his door, but I could see straight away that he couldn't remember why I was there. I told him I was there about my contract and he went: "Oh yes. Here's a contract, sign it."

I looked at the contract, which was normally an old-fashioned blue piece of paper, which had all the bonus schemes, appearance money and everything written on it. But this one was blank! He just told me to sign it and to trust him or fuck off and play for Barnsley. There were no negotiations, no agents.

I finally got a call to pick up the contract and was expecting about £750 per week. Cloughie just said: "Thank you for agreeing to work with me for the next three years young man."

I said: "No, it's a pleasure boss". When I looked I couldn't believe my luck because he had given me a contract worth £1,500 a week. I was amazed. He'd doubled the amount of money I wanted.

Before the FA Cup final in 1990, we travelled to Bisham Abbey on Thursday night, as all teams did. The gaffer revealed the team by writing it on a bit of paper torn from a magazine. He gave it to the skipper and he read it out at the back of the bus.

On another occasion we were at Norwich and there was no sign of Brian Clough. Ronnie Fenton took the team talk and he said the gaffer would be along shortly. We won 2-1 but there was still no sign of BC. Afterwards we found out he had been at Trent Bridge, back in Nottingham, watching the Test match instead. Like me, he loved his cricket.

On away games, we used to pick players up at a hotel near Sandiacre. One day I looked out of the window of the bus and was amazed to see the boss in a garden breaking roses off. Afterwards, he went to the front door and shoved money through the letter box to pay for them. We thought he had gone mad until he came on the bus, that is. He presented us all with a rose. "Give them to your lovely wife or mother for Mothers' Day and tell them it's from Brian," he said.

On other occasions he would have the coach pull in at East Midlands airport to watch the planes take off. "It won't be long before that is us, off to Cala Millor at the end of the season," he'd say.

Once, on a trip to Holland, the gaffer was listening to my Chubby Brown tape on the bus. We were having a right laugh. We played the game and got off the bus to go for the after-match meal when a guy with a big Afro hair-do came to show us the way. I started taking the mickey out of him, but the gaffer overheard me. Suddenly, he grabbed me by the scruff of the neck and marched me into the massive dining room.

He told this lady that I was to help serve the meals to every-one. She kitted me out in a white pinnie and I had to go round with a big tray, serving people. To say I was embarrassed would be putting it mildly. As you can imagine, the lads simply slaugh-tered me. Some were still mentioning it two or three years later.

My old Wales team-mate Dean Saunders is a great story-teller and one of his best involves the time he almost signed for Forest from Derby. He went to Alan Hill's house with his agent, Kevin Mason, and was shown into the lounge along with Archie Gemmill and Liam O'Kane. Brian Clough sat looking through the patio windows at Alan's superb garden.

BC said to Archie: "Ask him if he can play with our Nigel." Dean said that he could and that they would complement each other well. Archie said: "He says, yes he can boss."

BC said: "Archie sign the young man."

Kev Mason said they needed to talk because Dean had a lot of clubs interested in signing him. But Brian Clough said: "Archie, tell the fat bastard he might know facts and figures, but he knows sod all about football."

With that he went out through the patio doors into the garden and started picking flowers. He came back in, dropping soil onto Hilly's nice white carpet, and gave the flowers to Dean to give to his wife, Helen. By the time Dean got home he found Brian Clough had beaten him back and was making himself at home, drinking a cup of tea. But the gaffer had wasted his time for once. Dean signed for Liverpool for a record British fee of £2.9m instead and didn't arrive at the City Ground until 1991.

But one of the best Brian Clough stories involves poor old David Currie, who cost Forest a whopping £1m when they signed him from Barnsley. He was a good striker but had only scored one goal in four games when his career at the City Ground came to an abrupt end.

His second car was a purple Ford Capri. It was old and clapped out, but he'd had it a long time and he loved it. Unfortunately, he made the mistake of leaving it in the club car park when we went to training.

The gaffer turned up 15 minutes late, as usual, and shouted to Archie Gemmill to get all the lads in. We got into a big circle and BC stood there looking at the ground, one hand over his mouth the other holding his trusty squash racket. The dog was going crazy, as usual, chewing a pair of the lads' underpants. The conversation that followed was something like this.....

"Who owns that old car in my fucking car park," asked Cloughie.

Currie goes: "It's mine boss."

"And what's your fucking name son?"

"David Currie boss."

"And where are you from David Currie?"

"You signed me from Barnsley boss."

"That's where that idiot is from," Clough said, pointing at me. "David Currie, have you bought a house in the Nottingham area yet?"

"No boss, but I'm looking."

"Son, don't bother."

Two weeks later David Currie was on his way to Leicester.

Cloughie was at his best on a trip to Sweden. We were playing a duff local side and were 4-0 up. It was absolutely freezing – it was so cold the polar bears were wearing duffle coats – and we had six subs shivering on the bench.

The facilities there were very basic but they did at least have a hot-dog van. Suddenly the gaffer turned to Terry Wilson and told him to go to one of the skips in the dressing room, where he would find a bottle of Vodka and some plastic cups.

The gaffer divided it up, a shot in each cup, and then sent for six hot-dogs to go with it. "It's to keep you warm, because you are all going on," said Clough. It was incredible, even for him. I was amazed. But it certainly warmed us up.

There will never be another one like him, will there? Roy Keane did a forward roll after scoring the only goal against Norwich. He got a bollocking from BC for his trouble. "If you want to be a gymnast I'll put you in the circus with the lions," he said.

When Teddy Sheringham signed for Forest BC said to him: "Well played Edward" as he came off the field. "Please don't call me Edward," said Teddy. "Only my mum calls me that. Call me Teddy." "No problem Teddy, sorry about that," said BC. But as he left the gaffer said: "See you lads. See you Edward. Sorry you don't like being called Edward, do you Edward?"

I am in the record books for scoring the first own goal in the Premiership. I saved a header from Colin Hendrie I think it was, against Blackburn. But as I scrambled to recover, the ball hit me and I knocked it into the net. We lost 4-1 that day, but at least I saved a penalty from Kevin Gallon. I had asked before the match for permission to be dropped off on the way home, but I was scared to walk past the boss in case he had a go at me.

But, rather than travel all the way back to Nottingham, I finally plucked up the courage and walked towards the door. And what did BC do? He only stood up and kissed me and said: "Say hello to your mum and dad from me. Oh, and by the way, don't come in until Thursday. Have a few days back home and spend some time with your lovely parents." Typical of him, doing the opposite of what you were expecting. As I got off the bus he gave me the thumbs up at the window. I can see him now

I was gutted when Brian Clough retired. We all knew he was coming towards the end of the road and some people think he should have gone earlier, because the game was changing fast.

It was a sad day and one I will never forget. It must have been so hard for him to walk away from Forest, but his health was deteriorating. It was plain for all to see.

People were saying we had a mathematical chance of staying up if we beat Sheffield United at home and Ipswich away on the last day. But we knew we were down. We were on a bad run and couldn't see where the next win was coming from.

The bottom line was we had not been good enough. The league table didn't lie. But it wasn't the gaffer's fault. We let him, and the fans, down. He certainly wasn't a failure. How could a man that won two European Cups and achieved what he achieved be classed as a failure? RIP gaffer....

Brian Clough on a rare visit to training

Brian Clough and Del Boy down at Forest's training ground

One man was a great manager....one wasn't

A sad end, Brian Clough's last game in charge of Forest

This picture still sends a shudder down my spine

An emotional farewell to the City Ground faitful

Forest are 2-1 down – can the master pull it off again?

I think the police lady is about to get a kiss

Brian Clough handed me the ball after my Forest debut against Liverpool

CHAPTER THREE
Life at the City Ground

I joined Forest as a trainee in 1987 and went on to have 13 fantastic years at the City Ground. When I turned 17 with the youth team, I signed a full-time apprenticeship. I was getting paid £35 a week, getting my digs paid for and my expenses. In those days I had to clean the boots of Ian Bowyer and Steve Sutton. Bomber used to embarrass me in front of the rest of the lads and I had to call him "King Ian".

You might have heard that I've got a bit of a reputation as a drinker. But I didn't really start going out drinking until I got in the first team at Forest. I couldn't afford it for one thing.

You can't afford to go far when you are living in digs and have to be in bed for a certain time. I was in the club's hostel for two years where Tom and Olive looked after us brilliantly.

When I was just starting out with Forest, we played in a tournament in France. Nigel Jemson, Phil Starbuck and me were in Paris hanging around. The coaching staff said we could go for a walk but we had to be back in two hours. Being young and naive we, of course, headed for the nearest club, which was advertising dancing girls for five francs. How could we resist a bargain like that?

We went inside and it turned out to be a terrifying experience because the girls came and sat with us, ordering drinks at about £40 a time. We were the only three punters in there and when we tried to leave the big bouncer locked the door and demanded money from us. Of course, we couldn't pay.

They started getting aggressive at that point and in the end Phil had to pay with eurocheques or something fancy. We made sure we never made that mistake again.

We also went to a big tournament in Holland where we came

up against Ajax, Barcelona and Feyenoord, some top teams from around the world. I ended up winning the award for the best goalkeeper in the tournament. Believe it or not, there were even rumours that Barcelona were interested in signing me.

As soon as I got back to Nottingham, my first professional contract was waiting for me. I'd impressed so much that they decided to let a couple of the other goalkeepers that were ahead of me in the pecking order go. I was offered a contract, £100 a week, take it or leave it. Obviously, I snapped their hands off.

After I graduated from the Colts, my first game for the reserves was against Sheffield United, who had Billy Whitehurst upfront. He was the son of a miner, like me, and he knew I had played for Hoyland Town Jaguars. But that didn't stop the big fella scaring the crap out of me.

Just before a corner was being taken, he came up to me and said that if I came for the ball I would end up with a nose like his...broken.

Now Billy was hard. Vinnie Jones and Razor Ruddock both said he was the hardest striker they had ever played against. High praise indeed! The rumour was that he once had his nose sewn back on after a fight in a pub. During a match the stitches started coming out, so he had his nose stapled back on at half-time. Did I come for the corner? What do you think?

When I was an apprentice my dad was working as a market trader. At Christmas I used to bring slippers and aftershave in and flog them to the lads to make a bit of extra cash for myself. Stuart Pearce had a couple of pairs of slippers and suddenly the orders got bigger.

It was Pearcey who gave me the nickname of Norm. People think it had something to do with Norman Wisdom or the fat bloke from Cheers. But it was Pearcey who gave it me, because he thought I looked like former Manchester United striker Norman Whiteside and it stuck.

I think my first game with the first-team squad was a testimonial for a well-known local footballer, Arthur Oldham, at Keyworth's Platt Lane ground. We won 8-0 and I wore the No.10 shirt.

I was still living in digs, and was about fourth-choice 'keeper, when I made my debut against Liverpool on October 26, 1988, aged 18. Steve Sutton went down with 'flu and Hans Segers and Paul Crichton were out on loan at Wimbledon and Torquay respectively. Steve apparently had a temperature of 101 and couldn't even get out of bed, let alone play against Liverpool.

I'd called in for fish and chips on the way from my digs on Colwick Road and arrived at the ground about 5 o'clock to get everything clean for when the players arrived.

I was doing my apprenticeship duties, minding my own business, sweeping the corridors, cleaning the toilets, cleaning all the players' boots.

I was in my blue apprentice tracksuit in the boot-room when there was a shout from behind the door. I put my head around the corner and there was Brian Clough. The gaffer had a few choice names for me, even in those days – like Shithead, Barnsley and Imbecile. This shout was: Norm....Shithead....come here, I want you. Put your boots on, you're playing". Just like that. It was 7 o'clock and the game kicked off at 7.45. At first I thought he was taking the piss out of me again, just having a laugh at my expense.

Little did I know that earlier in the day he'd got someone to telephone my dad and let him know I was making my debut against the mighty Liverpool. He got my dad down to Nottingham and let him sit in the directors' box to watch his son play in his first, professional football game. Sadly, my mum, who had never missed a game, was on holiday in Torquay.

I only knew 45 minutes before the kick off. It was a great plan, great man management because he knew that I didn't have time to get nervous. I suddenly found myself sitting with Pearcey and Steve Chettle. Pearcey just told me I'd be fine and I was. I just went out there and played. I remember warming up, and Brian Rice said: "Come on. Let's go out, get a taste of the atmosphere, get a taste of the crowd. No-one is going to know who you are, just come out and I'll kick a few balls at you to get you warmed up." In those days there were no other 'keepers on the bench and it was the job of the sub to warm you up.

I was just coming back from a bad finger injury and the first ball Ricey kicked at me slipped straight through my hands and went into the net. Can you imagine what the crowd was feeling at the time? But they needn't have worried. Everything settled down and I had a fantastic game, not that I was ever nervous before a game. I was only sick on the pitch once and that was on the edge of the six-yard box at Chelsea.

To be honest, for some reason I was more nervous before a youth-team game or a reserve game than I ever was in the Premiership.

The crowd helped me a lot by applauding me onto the field. My first kick was a good one and I could hear the crowd gasp when they saw how far the ball went.

When I made my first save any nerves I might have had, left me straight away. It was a shot from England star John Barnes from 30-yards which swerved and dipped, but I dived and held it on the half volley. I couldn't believe I was out there facing the likes of Ian Rush, Peter Beardsley and Barnes.

It settled me down and I had no problems after that until Rush hooked one in from close range. All the pre-match hype had been about Rush, who was looking for a goal after coming back from Juventus, but that was the only time he got the better of Stuart Pearce, Des Walker and Colin Foster.

We had striker Lee Chapman making his home debut following his £300,000 move from France, but it was Rice and Neil Webb who got the all-important goals. We beat the mighty Liverpool 2-1 and after the game the manager got the match ball off the referee and presented it to me. He said: "Here's something that you can keep and treasure for the rest of your life."

He got everyone to sign it and I still treasure that ball to this day, although the autographs are starting to fade.

I kept my place in the team for the 1-0 win at Newcastle, Lee Chapman repaying a chunk of his transfer fee with the vital goal. He was an integral part of the Forest team that won the Littlewoods Cup and Simod Cup in 1989, scoring two goals in the Simod final against Everton at Wembley. He was married to the actress Leslie Ash and used to turn up in designer gear. He really loved himself, but I don't think he was anything really special.

Newcastle boasted Brazilian star Mirandinha and had Dave Beasant in goal. We rode our luck as Steve Chettle cleared one off the line and John Cornwall headed against the bar, but I didn't really have a lot to do until I made a crucial save with a couple of minutes to go.

I rushed off my line to clear the ball and when I got back to my feet all I could see was Brian Clough, on the bench, with his head in his hands. I think he was convinced I was going to give a penalty away. Afterwards I met up with my dad and my cousin Glenn. My dad was so proud of me. I'll never forget that look on his face that day.

I also played in the 3-2 League Cup win over Coventry at the City Ground. Colin Foster, Stevie Hodge and Nigel Clough got the goals and Gary Charles made his debut. The other thing I remember is that David Speedie kicked me on the head. Brian Clough collared him in the tunnel at half time and said: "If you kick my goalkeeper again I'll set my captain on you young man."

Speedie was as good as gold after that. The next time I met Speedie was at a PFA dinner when he turned up in jeans and a dickie bow. He unwisely came over to our table for a word and I thought Stan Collymore was going to lay him out.

The boss never said he was dropping me but I wasn't bothered because it was the right decision. I hadn't done too badly and we'd won all three games, but it was time to take me out of the firing line. I was too young; I was still learning my trade, but the boss now knew he could rely on me and throw me in at any time. More importantly, he knew he didn't have to go out and find another goalkeeper with Hans Segers – who was mad, by the way, even for a goalkeeper – out on loan.

A black day for football

I wasn't in the team that played Liverpool in the semi-finals of the FA Cup that disastrous day at Hillsborough in 1989. But I was standing on The Kop with my mates the day that 96 Liverpool fans lost their lives so tragically.

I got there late for some reason and the Kop end was packed tight and, at first, we thought it was just the Liverpool fans causing trouble. It was only when we saw people being carried onto the pitch on boards that we realised something was seriously wrong. Even then it didn't really sink in. My mum saw it on the news and rang to make sure I was all right.

On the way home we had the news on and began to realise what a massive tragedy it was..... 96 dead.

But this wasn't a plane crash or a terrorist bomb. This was just a football match. Twenty-two blokes kicking a bag of wind about.

There have been inquests and enquiries but I don't suppose we will ever know all the facts about what led to the tragedy or who was to blame.

The Forest players were all devastated. The whole place was flat and everyone who had been at the game was in a state of shock. How could you keep your mind on football after witnessing that? The rest of the season was a write-off and the replay was a non-event. It still chills me to think about it to this day....

The first step on the ladder with Nottingham Forest Colts

Pre-season training with Forest in 1987 - I wasn't that keen

The Nottingham Forest team line-up in 1987

On holiday in Cala Millor with Stoney, Jemmo and Woany

I was goalkeeper of the tournament in Holland. Lee Glover was the top scorer

We celebrate our win in Holland in 1987. Can you spot a young Gary Charles?

Back at the City Ground after we won the Groningen youth tournament in Holland for the second year running

I couldn't afford to buy any gloves so I borrowed these from Steve Sutton

Receiving the Barclays Young Eagle of the Year award

CHAPTER FOUR
Old Trafford here I come

I had to wait until November the following season for my next chance to shine and again it was a big one – Manchester United, live on television at Old Trafford. We lost 1-0. It helped me keep my place for the next five games.

We beat Manchester City 3-0 with two from Nigel Clough (one from the penalty spot) and Brian Rice. We pipped Everton 1-0 at home in the 4th round of the League Cup, Lee Chapman scoring from a free-kick awarded for time-wasting, and three days later we beat the Toffies 1-0 again at the City Ground with a Nigel Clough penalty. Stuart Pearce, Gary Crosby and Franz Carr were on target as Manchester City were beaten 3-2 in the Zenith Cup.

But December started badly with a 2-1 defeat at Villa. Steve Sutton came back in then and I had to wait until April for another game, but at least I won a new three-and-a-half year contract on the back of those six games when Steve Sutton was out.

Alex Ferguson must have been impressed with what he saw against Manchester United because he took me on loan for a month as cover for Scottish 'keeper Jim Leighton, after United failed to get a work permit for Mark Bosnich and Luton refused to extend Les Sealey's lone spell.

It came out of the blue and at first I thought it was wind-up. I'd been playing a third-team game at Scarborough when Archie Gemmill took me to one side on the bus and told me I was going to Old Trafford for a month. I just laughed. But it was no joke.

Cloughie had apparently upset United with some comments he made about them on television and was using me to help patch things up. The next day I was having dinner with the likes of Steve Bruce and Bryan Robson at The Cliff training ground. Can you believe that? I played four games for the reserves and kept three clean sheets. They looked after me superbly. Alex Ferguson was brilliant and I have always had great respect for him since then. It was an amazing place and you could get lost at The Cliff, it was so big. When you got changed you had to get in a mini bus to take you to the pitches.

It made Forest look a little small to say the least. I was shitting my pants because I didn't know what kind of reception I would get because there were some big-name players there even in those days. But I needn't have worried. Neil Webb was there, so at least I was assured of one friendly face and Mr Ferguson and all the players gave me a fantastic welcome.

Mike Duxbury would meet me at the motorway turn-off and I would follow him to the training centre. After two days I felt as though I had been there all my life. I trained with the first team, travelled with them and had a fantastic time.

It was absolutely superb training alongside stars like Bryan Robson and Mark Hughes. I played two games at Old Trafford in front of one man and a dog and, although it was a bit eerie, it was still brilliant. I was playing at Old Trafford and that was all that mattered. It was special, even if it was only for a month.

I travelled with the team for a cup game at Hereford and found myself playing cards with Gary Pallister, Brian McClair and Mr Ferguson. We were playing All Hearts, which was his favourite game, because it lasted about two hours and helped pass the time on trips. It wasn't for big stakes and I ended up winning £27, although, come to think of it, I never did get my winnings.

I could have stayed at Old Trafford for another month and I often wonder what would have happened if I had, because Jim Leighton was struggling for form and Les Seeley came into the side. If I had stayed I might have ended up playing in the Cup Final. You never know....

But I went back to Forest and Brian Clough put me straight back in the team. We came back to draw 2-2 at Liverpool after being two down after 13 minutes. It was a massive relief when Stevie Hodge and Nigel Jemson earned us a share of the points.

We then got our first win in nine games, 3-0 at Luton, but lost 2-0 at Southampton. Steve Sutton was back for the 1-0 League Cup final win against Oldham and made a great save, but I played in the superb 4-0 home win over Manchester United. Garry Parker, Stuart Pearce, Nigel Clough and Steve Chettle got the goals in a 25-minute blast.

In 1990, I got another big break when I was called up by Dave Sexton, along with Nigel Jemson, for the England U-21 side and we won the prestige Toulon tournament against Portugal, Russia and Czechoslovakia.

The gaffer came into the dressing room after a game at Mansfield and said: "Congratulations you two. You join up with the England team on Monday." Shocked? You bet I was. Sadly, Jemmo had to pull out after tweaking a hamstring. But we had a good side which included Carl Tiler, Tim Sherwood, Mark Robins, Lee Sharpe, Ian Olney and another 'keeper, Carl Muggleton. I played in three of the four matches in France and made some good saves against Czechoslovakia before we went on to win 2-1.

The Czech goal came from a penalty conceded by Oldham's Earl Barrett. We were not expected to do well and we lost our first match 1-0 to a very physical Portuguese side. But we bounced back to beat Russia 2-1 and thrashed France 7-3 with five goals from Mark Robins, who was with Manchester United at the time.

It was a great experience for me and made up, in a small way, for the disappointment of missing out on the Littlewoods Cup Final. You only got one cap a year in those days and I was very proud of mine, especially as I was one of the over-age players in the side.

I thought I had arrived and that things would take off from there, but, sadly, that was the end of my England career.

I made 38 League appearances for Forest that season and another 16 in the cups, a record I'm very proud of. And there was an added bonus when England boss Graham Taylor named me Barclays Young Eagle of the Year.

It was nice to get some recognition at that early stage of my career and it gave me a massive lift. I was shocked because it was unusual for 'keeper to be picked. That didn't happen often, especially with the likes of Matt Le Tissier, Rod Wallace and Mark Robins playing so well at the time. I thought I might get one of the regional awards, never the big one.

I was first-choice 'keeper at the start of the 1990-91 season with Steve Sutton's future at the club in doubt. I played in three pre-season friendlies and the County Cup final with Mansfield Town which we won 5-0. I set myself a target of 16 clean sheets and I never missed a match after that, 38 games in the League and 16 in cups. I had arrived, or so I thought.

But there were to be plenty of highs and lows along the way. Roy Keane made a shock debut in the 2-0 defeat at Liverpool and Coventry had three penalties in earning a 2-2 draw. Roy Keane opened his account in the 4-1 League Cup win over Burnley and David Howells grabbed a last-minute goal to give Spurs a 2-1 win. I managed to save a David Platt penalty to earn us a draw at Villa and we suffered our first League defeat at Derby since the 1979-80 season.

It was my first local derby and the atmosphere at the old Baseball Ground was electric, but the pitch was terrible. I remember I made a good double save from Paul Kitson, but I was gutted for the fans when we lost 2-1.

We also lost 5-4 in the League Cup at Coventry, despite a hat-trick from Nigel Clough. Incredibly, Coventry were 4-0 up after 34 minutes before we showed our character to battle back to 4-4. I had a poor game and started getting a bit of stick from the crowd. There were ironic cheers every time I caught the ball. But we had our revenge in January when we beat them 3-0 with goals from Clough, Pearce and Keane. Nigel actually missed a penalty in that match and Pearcey also wasted the re-take.

Our form in Division One had been a bit inconsistent and I was having a bad time. I was lucky to keep my place, to be honest. But we had been going well in the FA Cup and beat Palace 3-0 (following two draws).

We made hard work of beating them and the match was also postponed twice because of the weather. But it was our own fault because we let them off the hook at the City Ground. We were 2-1 up with a minute to go when Roy Keane passed the ball back to me from the half-way line.

Unfortunately, it fell short and I had to kick it away under pressure. But the ball fell to John Salako who chipped me. Brian Clough was waiting for us in the dressing room and when Roy Keane walked in he punched him the stomach. On the bright side, at least he left me alone this time!

We beat Newcastle 3-0, again after a replay. My mate Nigel Jemson bagged a hat-trick in the 3-1 win over Southampton and we pipped Norwich away with a goal from Roy Keane. That set up a semi-final tie with West Ham at Villa Park.

The atmosphere was unbelievable that day and the Hammers' fans in the Holte End were singing their heads off. But the game was all over as a contest when the Hammers had Tony Gale sent off by Keith Hackett for a professional foul near the centre circle on Gary Crosby, which would normally have been just a booking. I think it was the only time Gale was sent off in 700 games, so maybe it was a bit harsh.

The Second Division side were no match for us after that. We were such a good passing side that the ten men couldn't get the ball off us. I could have sat behind the goal and had a sing-song with the fans because I had so little to do.

The added bonus was that we were on an extra £5,000 if we

won. The fans thought Gary Charles kept giving me high-fives, but were were actually celebrating that extra £5k that was heading for our bank accounts. We were on a high now and hammered Chelsea 7-0, who had Dave Beasant in goal, and Norwich City 5-0 in successive home games.

Winger Gary Crosby scored a rare goal against Norwich to add to the one in the 6-2 win at Carrow Road earlier in the season. Gary, a bargain buy from Grantham, is best remembered for cheekily heading the ball out of Andy Dibble's hands and putting it in the net, but he was a good little player.

He had one trick which full-backs couldn't work out and a good long throw for a little lad. He was mates with Nigel Clough and I was pleased to see him go to Derby with Nigel from Burton Albion. But where did his hair go? We also pipped Leeds 4-3 with two each from Garry Parker and Nigel Clough, who also missed a penalty.

Remarkably, five days before the FA Cup Final, Brian Clough put a strong team out in a testimonial match for Mick Walker at Notts County. It was crazy, simply bananas. Only Brian Clough would gamble on doing something like that.

Anyway, we came though it without any injuries and we went down to Bisham Abbey on the Thursday ahead of the final. We didn't do any training, we just went for a walk and chilled out.

I had a steak and a beer. The gaffer didn't mind if you had a beer, as long as it was only one. I was rooming with Nigel Jemson but he had just been told he wasn't playing; in fact he wasn't even on the bench because there were only two subs in those days. I had to try and console him because he was obviously upset at missing out on the chance to run out at Wembley.

I slept in late on Friday morning and skipped breakfast. I was relaxed because I was convinced our name was on the cup, I really did. We wanted it so badly for the gaffer.

The only thing that stressed me was sorting out tickets for my mates and relatives, who were coming down by train. I had a chicken omelette and beans, it's what I fancied. Sometimes I would have beans on toast or a baked potato.

Time seemed to drag before we had to get on the bus in our posh sponsored suits and sponsored Ray-ban's. Suddenly, everyone wanted to sponsor you and the money all went into the players' pool. The fans were packing the streets, waving at us as we went by and everyone seemed so happy.

But there was no team talk from Brian Clough, no talk of tactics. There was no need. We knew what to do – head it or kick it when it came into the box, keep the ball on the ground, don't give it away and shoot when you get in the opposition box. You don't need to tell top players how to play. The boss just told us to go out and enjoy ourselves.

We lined up to meet Princess Diana, who was the main guest, and Pearcey had a £10 bet with me that she was wearing suspenders under her dress. I suppose he was just trying to relax me but, believe it or not, I was quite relaxed.

In the end we lost 2-1 and I made history by saving a Gary Lineker penalty but, believe me, that was no consolation for losing. It's a good job I saved the penalty because I was the guilty party; I brought Lineker down in the first place.

I thought I would be sent off for a professional foul and I screamed at referee Roger Milford that I'd got a touch on the ball (I still feel it wasn't a penalty, by the way). Fortunately, the referee didn't send me off; in fact he didn't even book me, which caused a bit of a stink at the time.

I was always confident when it came to penalties and that one was no different. I look at the DVD of the game now and think: "Did I really save that penalty?" But I'll let you into a little secret – I'd made up my mind which way to dive the day before. Gary hit the kick quite well, to my left, but it came at a nice height and I managed to block it.

But more people remember Dave Beasant because he was the first man to do it, when he saved John Aldridge's kick against

Liverpool in 1988. Everything was going our way. We were favourites with the bookies and I thought it was going to be our day after Gazza had got himself injured in a rash tackle.

Gazza was really hyped up; you could see it in his eyes. Stuart Pearce fired us in front from a trademark free-kick into the top corner and we could have gone 2-0 up when Gary Crosby went one-on-one with Erik Thorstvedt. At half time I was thinking: "Just 45 minutes to go and I'm a hero." But it wasn't to be.

They suddenly started to get on top of us after Gazza went off. Paul Stewart scored to take it into extra time and then Des Walker famously diverted the ball into his own goal. To be fair, he had to go for the ball. I shouted "Away" because it was too far for me to come, but it ended up in the net.

We were gutted, because we desperately wanted to win for the boss and nobody wanted to go to the after-match party. Brian Clough didn't say too much. He just said: "Well done lads, you gave your all."

I think he might have retired there and then if we had won. It was bitterly disappointing at the time ....it still is. I should have played in five cup finals at Wembley but, for varying reasons, I only played there once which remains a major disappointment for me.

Once you have played at Wembley it is like a drug. When you hear the national anthem it makes the hairs on the back of your neck stand up. It still does....

I get my hands on the Littlewoods Cup

Cloughie's badge said the world's greatest grandad

Not this time. I turn over a shot in the FA Cup final

Roy Keane helps me make a vital save from Paul Allen

A painful moment as I go down injured after crashing into a post

History in the making. I save a penalty from Gary Lineker at Wembley

Stuart Pearce helps me shut out Spurs and England striker Gary Lineker

Stunned by Des Walker's own goal at Wembley

A close call, but you need luck as a 'keeper

Facing the fans back home in Nottingham – remarkably, around 15,000 turned up even though we had lost

I was sponsored to wear Joe Bloggs clothes – not the worst fate in the world....

Yes, it's me in a Manchester United shirt

Three Lions on my chest in an England U-21 shirt

CHAPTER FIVE
I take some hammer

Forest began the 1991-92 season in Division One with a side I thought would be hard to beat with a back four of Gary Charles, Stuart Pearce, Des Walker and new boy Carl Tiler operating behind Roy Keane, Gary Crosby, Scot Gemmill, Nigel Clough, Nigel Jemson and Teddy Sheringham, who had arrived from Millwall for a club record £2m. Teddy oozed class and bagged 20 goals in 53 appearances in that first season as we finished eighth in Division One.

I enjoyed playing behind Carl Tiler, you could always rely on him winning the ball in the air. But he had a strange habit of looking down at his feet every time the ball went out of the play. Maybe he was just checking to make sure they were still attached to the end of his legs. Whatever the reason, it used to drive Brian Clough mad. He used to shout: "Tiler, stop looking at your feet or I will chop your balls off."

We once played a reserve game at Barnsley and BC was in the stands. You could hear him shouting: "Tiler, stop looking at your feet" as clear as a bell. Incidentally, Carl was a brilliant cricketer, a fast bowler and good batsman. I reckon he could have made a living out of the game if he hadn't been a foot-baller.

One of the young lads at the club was a striker called Jason Kaminsky. He only made one first-team start before being released, sadly, he drank himself to death. Apparently, he took Brian Clough's death hard and died of liver failure after spending eight weeks in hospital. He was just 31.

Anyway, we made a good start with a 2-1 home win over Everton, but then typically lost 1-0 at Leeds. I was looking forward to the next game, at Notts County, and we got back on track with a 4-0 win over our near neighbours. I remember that Roy Keane pulled one back for Teddy Sheringham to tap and in Gary Charles burst into the box and smashed one in.

Gary was a great little player who should have been the England full-back for many years to come and was a better defender than Glen Johnson will ever be. I played in the same Colts side as Gary, even though I was a bit older. He was a great lad but had personal troubles off the pitch that got the better of him after he followed Steve Sutton to Derby for £750,000.

He wasn't mentally strong enough and ended up in trouble with the police after his career fizzled out through injury at West Ham. It was a great waste of talent.

Scot Gemmill was also a good little player. It was probably hard for him, following in his dad's footsteps at the City Ground. Like me, he had a few hard times and took some stick from the crowd. But, to be fair, he never hid. He always wanted the ball.

Scot wasn't a big eater and his dad used to come over and make sure he finished his meals, because he wanted him to bulk up a bit. Fortunately, I sat next to him and he used to push his food on to my plate when his dad wasn't looking.

Roy Keane was starting to get a few goals, with two in the 4-2 home win over Wimbledon, but we couldn't get a consistent run going. We put five past Bolton in the League Cup, but then lost 4-2 at Sheffield United and 3-1 at home to Southampton. But we had our revenge over them in the League Cup, knocking them out 1-0 after a replay. Then Des Walker scored his only goal for Forest, in the 1-1 home draw with Luton Town. Ironically, Steve Sutton was in goal for Luton that day.

There was certainly nothing wrong with our cup form and we beat Wolves, Hereford and Bristol City in the FA Cup, but Crystal Palace proved more troublesome in the 5th round of the League Cup. We drew 1-1 at their place but put four past them in the replay thanks to a hat-trick from Teddy Sheringham.

Leicester were dumped out of the semi-final of the Zenith

Cup 2-0 after a replay and we booked another trip to Wembley after pipping Spurs 2-1 in the semi-finals of the League Cup.

We were drawn away to Portsmouth in the 5th round of the FA Cup but I had other things on my mind at that time. My career was in jeopardy after I spent a night in the cells following a spot of bother in Barnsley, which I will go into later. I should have pulled out of the game, because I had other things on my mind. But I went ahead and played – with disastrous results.

We lost 1-0 and it was my fault. Darren Anderton put a cross in and it was a simple take from my point of view.

But I fumbled it and left a simple tap in. I was shell-shocked, but I was still confident we would win. Unfortunately, Alan Knight was in inspired form as we battered them.

In the second-half I had to go to the end where the Forest fans were and they weren't happy with me – to put it mildly. I could have picked up twenty-five quid in loose change after they started pelting me with coins.

People were saying I had to get away from Forest and make a fresh start. Some fans would probably have given me a lift down there and paid for the petrol themselves. They hated "Calamity Crossley" that much. They were writing to the local newspaper, the Nottingham Evening Post, calling me a clown and all sorts of hurtful things. It was calamity this and calamity that and suddenly everybody wanted to see the back of me.

But I never got angry about it. What's the point? It just made me more determined to prove them wrong. My heart was in the club and I never ever thought about quitting. That's not in my nature.

Maybe I was thrown in at the deep end too soon, who knows? There's not a 'keeper born who hasn't made a mistake. But when you are a 'keeper, one slip can destroy your confidence, your reputation and your future. Peter Bonetti kept six clean sheets in his first six games for England. Then he threw in one goal and never played for his country again. And just look at what happened to Robert Green in the last World Cup.

The main thing is to buckle down, work hard, learn from it and make sure it doesn't happen again. I watched videos of the goals I let in and I always felt that I might have done better with some of them. I played in the 2-0 wins over Coventry and Norwich, but I was then banned from the ground for two weeks following my brush with the law.

I kept myself ticking over back home with my mum and dad, but even they grounded me! Andy Marriott took my place for the next eight matches and I was left kicking my heels with nothing to do.

I wasn't worried about getting my place back because, without being big-headed, I knew I was a better 'keeper than Andy. The lads used to hammer him and he took a lot of stick for the kind of gear he used to wear.

But, just in case, I sent my dad down to spy on him. The feedback wasn't good from my point of view.

"He did very well. He's a good 'keeper" was my dad's honest assessment after Forest beat Manchester United 1-0 and Manchester City 2-0. It was hard sitting watching him play in the 3-2 Zenith Cup final win over Southampton and he still had the League Cup final with Manchester United to come.

This was a far worse punishment than anything the courts inflicted on me. Liam O'Kane pulled me to one side and dropped a strong hint that the gaffer was thinking about bringing me back against United and I had a gut feeling that he would.

I felt he would want to field his strongest side – but he didn't. Maybe he should have because I think I might have stopped the winning goal from Brian McClair.

I went down to the game but don't remember too much about it. I was probably too busy sulking. It should have been me out there but it wasn't Andy's fault, it was mine.

I had nobody to blame but myself. The boss put me straight back in after the cup final and I played in the final six games of the season as we finished eighth in the league – but that was no consolation at missing out on the thrill of two cup finals.

Football changed forever at the start of the 1992-93 season when the Premiership was formed. Even though Des Walker, Steve Hodge and Terry Wilson had gone, the fans said we were too good to go down. They were wrong. I thought Brian Clough would work his magic and put things right, but his health was starting to deteriorate.

To make matters worse, my form was up and down as we went ten games without a win after beating Liverpool 1-0 at the start of the season with a goal from Teddy Sheringham.

It was the first live Premiership game ever televised by Sky. Sadly, Teddy left soon afterwards and we lost six games in a row. Teddy said he wanted to move back to London with just three games gone. There were plenty of rumours and he got some stick from the lads before he left.

I threw one in during the 4-1 defeat by Blackburn to earn the dubious honour of becoming a pub quiz question: "Which player conceded the first own goal in the Premier League?"

Yes it was me. It had crossed my mind that I would have to find another club because of the pressure I was under. For a lad of my age I thought I had done pretty well, but more and more fans were starting to take the piss.

Alan Hill did his best to get me through the worst of it. But things got so bad that even my mother wouldn't speak to me until she found out the result of our game on television.

But I was determined not to give in to the boo boys. It would have been easy to knock on the boss's door and ask to be left out. But I was determined to see it through.

A mate of mine, Stan Mitchell, said the best thing I could do was go and face the fans at the Crown pub in The Meadows, in Nottingham. I thought about it for a while and finally took the plunge one Sunday dinner. I got a bit of stick when I first walked in with Stan riding shotgun. The lads were flinging beer mats and shouting: "Catch. Don't drop it," stuff like that. But, after a pint or two, I became their new best friend and it became a regular Sunday haunt of mine.

We finally beat Middlesbrough 1-0 with a goal from Kingsley Black and I kept a clean sheet in the draw at Sheffield United after I made a great save at the feet of my old mate Vinnie Jones. It made me feel a lot better, but we were still 22nd in the League and in for a hard season. The simple fact was, we were leaking goals and not scoring enough at the other end.

Neil Webb was back. He is a kindred spirit. Like me he had a bit of trouble with his weight occasionally, but he was that good he didn't have to run about. You don't get to play for England and Manchester United by being a bad player do you?

He scored goals from midfield, a quality player who timed his run into the box well. He was one of the lads and we all got on with him.

Robert Rosario and Gary Bannister came in up front in place of Teddy. Gary actually wrote to Brian Clough and asked him to sign him. I think the gaffer liked that and gave him a chance. He had a good record as a striker but, to be fair, his best days were behind him and I didn't think he was up to Premier standard. He was certainly no Teddy Sheringham for a start and I think one of his legs was two inches shorter than the other as the result of a childhood accident.

As I have said before, we used to have some fun in Jersey. One night we had a bad dress night and we wondered what had happed to Gary Bannister. When he finally emerged from his room he had built a crane with tooth picks stuck in the gaps in his teeth and it was hanging from his mouth. It must have taken him hours to make it. He was a funny guy.

Perhaps we thought we were better than we were, I don't know. But I do know that the league table never lies and we won only eight more League games all season. We lost 4-3 at QPR and I was having a bad one. Ron Fenton stormed into the dressing room at half time and, in front of all the lads, told the gaffer to get me off. I never had a problem with Ron and this wasn't like him. I thought I was being made a scapegoat, after all there are eleven men in a team. But passions were running high at the time.

Anyway, I was dropped for the first time (for loss of form) and Andy Marriott came in for the last five games of the season, which produced just one win, 2-1 at home to Spurs thanks to goals from Kingsley Black and Robert Rosario.

Kingsley had a good touch, but he was no world beater. He was very quiet and hardly said a word – until we got a few beers in him and then he would open up.

Rosario, with his size 14 feet, held the ball up well and flicked it on. But he was not a great scorer of goals, which was what we needed at the time. In fact, he only scored three goals in 28 appearances for Forest and retired to go into coaching at the age of 29 after a cruciate ligament injury.

Defeats to Wimbledon and Sheffield United sealed our fate. I wasn't involved in the game with The Blades and I'm glad I didn't play. All I remember is the sadness, the dressing room was like a morgue and not a lot was said.

When he walked out onto the pitch all the fans, even the Sheffield supporters, were singing "There's only one Brian Clough."

I couldn't believe this was the last day we would see the back of the famous green shirt at the City Ground. He never said goodbye to us individually, in fact I don't recall him saying much at all. But it was an emotional moment and a few tears were shed, I can tell you.

Brian Clough's final game was away to Ipswich, which we lost 2-1. I travelled to Portman Road with the lads even though I wasn't playing. I wanted to be part of his last day. But, again, it was very sad. To be frank, it was shit in the end, we finished rock bottom, four points adrift of Middlesbrough, and were relegated. We couldn't even find any comfort in the cups, losing 2-0 to Arsenal in the fifth round of both the Coca Cola Cup and FA Cup. Nigel Clough was Forest's top scorer in the League with just ten league goals..... and three of those were penalties!

It said it all really. It was such a shame it ended that way. And it's a crime the gaffer never got to manage England when he was in his prime. Who knows, we just might have ended up winning the World Cup.....

Forest's Zenith Data Systems Cup winning squad in 1991-92

I congratulate my rival, Andy Marriott, after the 3-2 ZDS Cup final win

I didn't play in the Cup final, but I was still part of it all

Despair after the 3-0 home defeat by Norwich City in 1993

Dedicated followers of fashion....more like Rupert Bear

I let the team down at Portsmouth after my brush with the law

I was never a big fan of pre-season training as you can probably tell

CHAPTER SIX
Life without Brian Clough

Many people at the City Ground wanted Martin O'Neill to replace Brian Clough. But, in the end, Forest old boy Frank Clark, who had done a great job at Orient, was the man charged with reviving Forest's fortunes. He was BC's choice and he had Alan Hill as his No.2, which delighted me.

But, even then, it was still hard to believe that Brian Clough had gone after 18 years at the helm. Frank had some big shoes to fill and his job wasn't helped by the departure of two star players, Roy Keane and Nigel Clough, while Gary Charles went to Derby County.

But Frank pulled off a masterstroke when he persuaded Stuart Pearce to stay and signed Stan Collymore, from Southend. Stan might have had a bit of a reputation, but he certainly knew the way to goal and repaid Frank with 24 of them, 19 in the league, in his debut season.

As well as Stan, Frank also brought in Colin Cooper (Millwall), Des Lyttle (Swansea), David Phillips (Norwich City), World Cup star Lars Bohinen (Lillestrom) and Jason Lee (Southend). They all turned out to be good signings in their own way and I don't think Frank ever got the credit he deserved for that.

Dave Phillips was so versatile he could play in three or four positions – at the same time! He was technically very good and scored some great goals, but he was also boring. He would have sent a glass eye to sleep. Honest, he would.

I'd never heard of Des Lyttle until he popped up on the pre-season trip to Italy. He's a cheeky little chappie and a great lad. I played a bit of golf with him. He thinks I'm mad by the way.....he's probably right.

I remember when Stan Collymore first arrived and we went to Italy. We went to a restaurant down the road from our headquarters for all our meals. It was a nice stroll especially walking back after an evening meal of pasta and pasta and more pasta. But the next minute, while we were waiting for the meal to be served, a scrap suddenly broke out. Stan and big bad Rob Rosario came to blows. I don't know what sparked it off. I suppose Stan wanted to let everyone know who was 'The Man', even though it was evenly matched before the lads dived in and pulled them apart. They shook hands and left it at that.

Punches were also thrown on the training ground. Big Alfie Inge-Haaland was marking Stan one morning and Alfie was getting a little bit tight to Stan and niggling at his ankles. To be fair to Stan he did say: "Alfie, it is just training but if you kick me again I'll smack you." True to his word, as the ball was up the other end of the pitch Stan laid Alfie out. You should have seen the size of Alfie's lip. Sorry Alfie, you deserved that one.

A lot is made of it in the press when players have a bust-up on the training ground or in the dressing room. But it wasn't unusual in those days. Things would often kick off in the heat of the moment. Usually, it was just handgbags, a bit of pushing and shoving, that helps relieve the tension. I wish it happened more these days, but it doesn't.

It's a fact of life that some players just don't get on. Andy Cole and Teddy Sheringham, strike partners at Manchester United, apparently hardly spoke a word to each other off the pitch. But we all got on well at Forest, apart from Des Walker and Brian Laws, who had a bit of history.

It all kicked off at a training camp in Bordeaux. We were in log cabins behind a hotel and I was sharing a room with Terry Wilson. I was happy because I used to be in digs with him in Colwick Road in Nottingham. I heard a noise and found Des and Brian coming to blows behind one of the cabins.

Des was getting the worst of it, so I raced over, rugby-tackled

Brian and pulled him off. As usual on these trips someone, fed by boredom, thought it would be fun to put Brian's bed in the bath, just for a laugh. But Brian didn't see the funny side of it and blamed Des, who ended up with cuts and bruises. The gaffer must have known what went on, but he turned a blind eye to it.

John Sheridan, who had only been with us for about a week, must have wondered what he had walked into, especially after some of us sneaked over the wall for a night out on the town. Let's just say that things got a bit out of hand and we played follow my leader all the way back to base, doing a bit of damage to a few cars along the way.

And I'll never forget the day Des Walker had a bust-up with Franz Carr on the team bus. For some reason Des decided to put a hot spoon on Franz's neck. Unfortunately, it was so hot that it stuck to his skin. Franz wasn't happy, to say the least, and there was a bit of handbags for a while.

Team bonding sessions can also sometimes go wrong as I know to my cost. Once, in Jersey, Ian Woan was winding me up. I warned him to stop, but he carried on and pushed me too far. The red mist came down and I ended up breaking my nose on his head! It would not stop bleeding but I felt no pain! Obviously, I'd had a few, as you do on these trips.

In Jersey, they banned dancing in nightclubs on Sunday nights for some reason, can you believe that? Anyway we were in a club, which was pretty packed, apart from the deserted dance-floor when Garry Parker suddenly dived on it and started break-dancing on his own. It was hilarious. The last we saw of him was when two bouncers picked him up and escorted him out.

We used to stay at the Grand Hotel in Jersey, which really was a grand hotel. It was so posh they had little dips on the bar for the punters.

One night we went out for an Indian meal and I thought it be good fun to get some of the hottest curry they had and put it in the dips. The curry sauce, by the way, was impossible to eat. It would have taken the enamel off your teeth. It was like having a razor blade on your tongue. But how much fun did we have watching people try the dip? Later we found Alan Hill's room number and ordered a bottle of the most expensive champagne the hotel had, on his bill of course! Childish I know. But it was good fun.

On another occasion Roy Keane had a run-in with lady hockey player. She wanted him to sign a pair of her knickers but, for some reason, she ended up throwing a drink over him and he threw his pint over her. Happy days!

In January, I had signed a new four-year deal along with Ian Woan and Scot Gemmill, who had also been getting some stick from a section of the fans.

That year I was arrested after an attack on a man in Hoyland. Forest weren't happy, to say the least, and I faced a two-week ban. Hardly the the best of starts under new manager Frank Clark. It was my 24th birthday and Frank tore the fine up in front of me, which was good of him.

But I thought my days were numbered when he was linked with a move for Tommy Wright. It was doing my head in. After all, a player of Tommy's calibre wasn't coming to sit on the bench as a No.2 was he?

But it was probably just the kick up the backside I needed. After all, Andy Marriott had hardly pushed me, had he? But Tommy Wright? That was a different kettle of fish.

We started the season with a 1-1 draw against Southend and fans were throwing plastic hammers onto the pitch in reference to my recent court case. Even I had to see the funny side of that.

But it was no laughing matter when I had to have seven stitches in my forehead at half-time (with no anaesthetic) after diving at the feet of Andy Sussex. They wanted to take me off, but I carried on with a massive bandage around my bonce.

I don't remember much about it. All I remember is looking up and seeing the ball go in the net and feeling the blood running into my eye. I didn't even know a goal had been given until I got back on my feet. I was concussed, I suppose, but there was no way I was going off on a stretcher. I felt dizzy and had a bit of pain in my head, but I didn't see any reason to come off. I'd got Andy Marriott breathing down my neck for a place in the side. There was also talk of Forest going after the highly-rated American Brad Friedel. I got a shock when I turned up for training one day and saw Brad there. He looked the part even then. But, fortunately for me, the club couldn't get a work permit for him at the time.

They say you have to be mad to be a 'keeper. I don't know about that, but it certainly helps. OK, so I had a bit of a headache but you can't afford to give it a second thought when you are in goal. Hesitate and the ball can end up in the back of the net.

Next up was the big match with Derby County. There was no way I was going to miss that one and I ran out with a special padding, designed by physio Graham Lyas, to protect the stitches. We drew with the Rams and then put five past Grimsby, but struggled to put a run together. We were held 3-3 in the League Cup at Wrexham, despite a hat-trick from Stan Collymore, and Tommy took my place following his £450,000 move from Newcastle. Tommy's first game was at Bolton and Forest lost 4-3.

I must admit that, just for one brief moment, I was glad Tommy had let four in, but I'd have been happier if we had won 5-4. Yes, I actually wanted him to flop. How else was I going to get my place back in the side? We then drew 1-1 with Portsmouth thanks to a goal from Steve Stone.

Stoney was younger than me, but I took to him straight away. He was a central midfield player and stood out for me, but he never really got a look-in because of the form of Scot Gemmill.

As a result Stone was eventually converted to a right winger, but it worked out well for him and he went on to play for England. We called him Bulldog at Forest, but not because of the way he used to chase after players and tackle them. It was because he made grunting noises, just like a dog, when he was playing – and eating for that matter! He had a house and an apartment in Marbella and he let me have his apartment. One day my son Tommy was ill and Stoney's lovely wife, Judith, looked after him and gave him some Calpol. Of all the players' wives, I really liked and trusted her. I'm pleased to see him doing so well at Newcastle. He's very knowledgeable about the game.

Frank circulated to other clubs that both Andy Marriott and myself could go out on loan, following Tommy's arrival. He had a chat with us and said he wanted us to be playing in front of big crowds rather than languishing in the reserves, so that we would be sharp and ready when we came back.

I had made over 100 appearances since taking over from Steve Sutton, but I was still getting some abuse from a few supporters, which was a bit disappointing.

A 'keeper needs confidence. I can understand their frustration, but it was only making matters worse. You have to try and ignore it and get on with the game. That's the trouble when you are the last line of defence. You can be the hero one minute and a villain the next. I was having trouble with crosses, but I came in for special training so that I would be 100% when my chance to shine came again.

Lars Bohinen, who cost a bargain £450,000, made his debut in the 3-0 win at Birmingham which sparked an unbeaten run of 14 games. Coincidence? I don't think so. Lars was that good. Lee Glover, who had played with me in the Colts, got two of the goals.

Lee had a good touch and was the first footballer I came across who was really intelligent. He finished second in the Britain's brainiest footballer competition. I hadn't seen him for years, but bumped into him when I was doing my 'A' licence in Ireland. I couldn't believe he was on the same course. What's the chances of that? Brian Clough loved him because he could hold a ball and turn with it. But he was never a big crowd favourite for some reason. Perhaps they expected him, as a striker, to score more goals. He scored only nine in 76 games before being sold to Port Vale.

I finally got back in the side in unfortunate circumstances when Tommy Wright's son was taken ill. Andy Marriott had been sold to Wrexham and I was in the reserves, but I never let my head drop; never let it get me down. I came back at West Brom and we won 2-0 with two from Stan Collymore. Tommy was back for the 3-2 win at Sunderland, but he came off injured early doors. I replaced him and we won 3-2, with two more from Stan.

When Forest played Barnsley at the City Ground we arranged to go out to a nightclub after the match. I had about ten lads staying at my place which was only two up two down. Back at my place, Gerry Taggart and Steve Birdekin played a trick on Andrew Horsfield, who was my best mate from school. He woke up the next day with a hangover – minus his eyebrows, which had been shaved off in the night.

Steve Guinan and Lee Stratford were staying with me at the time. I was not on a lot of money and they rented a room off me. Two of my old mates, Carl 'Nog' Pickering and Gary 'Tat' Hurst, 'borrowed' some of Steve's designer gear for a joke and were last seen walking round Barnsley in it. They must have been the only people in Barnsley wearing Prada and Armani. They never said anything to me about it and I told Steve we must have been burgled. Sorry Steve!

I played for the rest of the season and felt as though I was ecapturing my best form. I was even coming for crosses and the fans were finally back on my side. We went ten games without defeat and went on to finish second behind Crystal Palace. Quite an achievement.

In fact, we clinched promotion with two games to go after

winning 3-2 at Peterborough. We had to come back from 2-0 down after seven minutes with two more from Stan and a rare Stuart Pearce header. The support from the Forest fans was amazing that day, so many turned up at London Road that they could not pack them all in. They were hanging from the floodlights and invaded the pitch after we scored the third goal. The last game of the season was at Mansfield and I blasted in a penalty in a 3-3 draw.

Amazingly, we were back in the Premier League. What's more we had the hugely-talented Bryan Roy partnering Stan Collymore upfront. It was a dream combination.

They were great individual talents, but together they were amazing and scored 40 goals between them as we shocked the football world by finishing third behind Blackburn Rovers and Manchester United.

Our tactic was simple. Soak up the pressure and get the ball to Stan as quickly as possible. And it worked. It was remarkable; unthinkable. We were tipped to go straight back down by some people. But it was no fluke, I can tell you. I'd first seen Roy in the Ajax youth team and he was quality. God knows how Frank managed to get him to sign for Forest from Foggia for £2.9m. Stan came with a bad reputation, but Frank just let him get on with it. He was happy as long as he was scoring goals. Stan was last in for training and first away; not that he was a great trainer anyway. But you could always tell when Stan wasn't playing because we didn't score!

No one could quite believe it as we went eleven games without defeat. I was even pinching myself and started to get superstitious. If we won a game I would keep the same shirt. If I played well I would make a point of wearing the same gloves again. It seemed to work as we put four past both Sheffield Wednesday and Spurs, but a 2-0 defeat at home to Blackburn Rovers (who else?) saw us go six games without a win. I hate playing against Blackburn. I should have said to the gaffer: "You might as well leave me out and play someone else because we are never going to win with me in goal."

A bad kick from me saw us lose 1-0 at Liverpool, which was unusual because I normally had a good kick. Apart from that I thought it was one of my best displays in a Forest shirt. We won 2-1 at Manchester United with goals from Stan and Pearcey and put four past Ipswich and Leicester before we ended the season with 13 games without defeat. That included a magnificent 7-1 win at Sheffield Wednesday, when Bryan Roy and Stan Collymore were on fire.

Wednesday were managed by Trevor Francis at the time and they had Des Walker, John Sheridan and Chris Bart-Williams in their side. But it wouldn't have mattered if Jose Mourinho had been their boss, because no one could have lived with us that day. We were that good!

I only touched the ball once and that was to pick it out of the back of the net. I was leaning against a post most of the time having some banter with the fans behind the goal. They were shouting "Norman, Norman what's the score?" But maths isn't my strong point and I must admit, I lost count after four.

I ended up playing all 42 League games, plus six in the cups, that season and kept 13 clean sheets. I had never played better and I think I was as good as anybody in the league that year.

I was maturing and making fewer mistakes, but I was having trouble with my weight.

That's why I always liked to wear black, because it made me look thinner. Well, that's the theory anyway. I'm a big eater, I admit it, I like my grub. I should have kept my eye on it, but I was dining out too much; getting through too many take-aways and junk food. It wasn't the booze. I never drank in the house, apart from the odd glass of wine.

But I did like my nights out though – the foreign lads thought we were crazy. But I didn't overdo it, perhaps ten Buds and a couple of shots to celebrate a win or drown my sorrows, depending on the result of the game.

Liam O'Kane used to weigh us every Friday. I could never understand a word he said, by the way. He used to stand over the players – especially me. I would do everything in my power to cheat the scales. I would stand on one leg to distract him and then put one hand on the table to take the weight off. Sometimes I would try and nudge the weight along until the day the club bought some new electronic scales. I was devastated and Liam couldn't understand how I'd managed to put about two stone on almost overnight!

That Monday I started my first diet. I've been on about 290 Monday diets since then! When I joined Forest, I weighed 13st 9lbs, when I left I weighed 15st 10lb. I'd always had trouble keeping my weight down, but I'd obviously put on a bit of muscle over the years.

It certainly came as a shock to the system when I signed for Middlesbrough, because I suddenly realised how much the game had moved on in the 13 years I had been at the City Ground, in terms of training, diet and conditioning.

At Forest we played on a Saturday and the gaffer would say: "See you on Tuesday." Even then, we didn't train much. As a result, pre-season was always very hard. I hated it. I dreaded it. But it was a whole new world at 'Boro with individual fitness coaches and I never had a problem with my weight. Honest!

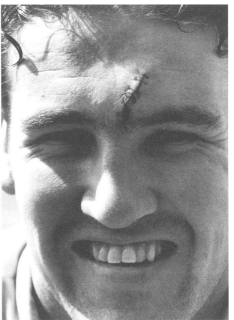

You don't have to be mad, but it helps   *It's a right stitch up after I was injured*

The Nottingham Forest squad which did so well with Frank Clark at the helm

Celebrating promotion with Forest in 1994 with Ian Woan

The Forest players celebrate a return to the top flight

Simple Simon says put your hands on your head....

Clock the fancypre-season foot work

CHAPTER SEVEN
Europe Here We Come

Despite our success the previous season, which earned us qualification for the UEFA Cup, we couldn't hold on to super Stan Collymore, who was off to Liverpool for a British record fee of £8.5m. Italian international striker Andrea Silenzi came in from Torino, along with Chris Bart-Williams (Sheffield Wednesday) and Kevin Campbell (Arsenal).

Kevin Campbell was good, but he was no Stan, while Silenzi had been leading scorer in Serie A and had played with Maradona at Napoli. I think I'm right in saying that he was the first Italian to play in the Premiership. Sadly, he was a flop at Forest. It was shame because he was a nice lad, but he couldn't hit a barn door. Quite frankly, he was shit. His nickname was 'Big Brush' because he was so tall. Unfortunately, he was also as daft as a brush and he was so clumsy that he kept falling over his own feet, even in training.

He only made a handful of appearances in three seasons at the City Ground. But one good thing did come out of his stay – he taught me how to say 'toothpick' in Italian, which came in handy when I was ordering a steak.

Nevertheless, the season kicked off well as we beat Southampton 4-3 away with two from Bryan Roy and went twelve games without defeat (24 if you count the previous season).

But the run came to an end in devastating fashion when we were hammered 7-0 at Blackburn. Alan Shearer bagged a hat-trick and just to rub salt into the wounds, Lars Bohinen, who had been sold for £700,000, scored twice.

I've blanked most of it out, but I do remember a Graeme Le Saux free-kick that hit the bar, bounced down on the line and ended up in the net. It was one of the darkest moments of my career and, as if that wasn't bad enough, they also did us 5-1 at the City Ground.

Now you can see why I hated playing against Blackburn Rovers and Alan Shearer in particular. On his day he was scary. He had everything, pace, a powerful shot, he was good in the air and was brave with it as well.

I was at a low ebb, but I felt I had to face the fans, so I went into The Crown pub in the Meadows area of Nottingham to see the 'A' Block lads. They broke the ice by buying me a crate of Seven Up! We bounced back to draw 1-1 at home to Manchester United and also drew the next three matches by the same score against Bolton, Villa and Manchester City.

Liverpool put four past us and we were thumped 5-0 at Premier League champions Manchester United, who banged in goals through Paul Scholes, David Beckham (2), Ryan Giggs and Eric Cantona, who sent me the wrong way from the penalty spot. Jason Lee and Bryan Roy were our top scorers with just eight league goals. So, in the end, I suppose we did well to finish ninth. Incredibly, I managed to stay injury free and made a total of 55 league and cup appearances.

We had a good run in the FA Cup, beating Spurs 3-1 on penalties before losing 1-0 to Villa in the 6th round. I grabbed the headlines against Spurs after managing to save penalties from Clive Wilson, Ronny Rosenthal and Teddy Sheringham. I don't think Alan Sugar was too happy with me when I attempted to celebrate with a Klinsmann dive. I just belly-flopped and left a big dent in his pitch. Rumour has it that the crater I left could be seen from the moon!

We did even better in Europe where we were the surprise package, despite having such a small squad. Playing in Europe was totally different. The pace was slower for one thing and you had to learn to adapt quickly. But, fair play to Frank, he got his tactics spot on.

In the UEFA Cup, we drew Malmo in the first round and went through on the away goal rule. We were up against Auxerre in the next round and were again the massive underdogs. We were having a pre-match meal before the game in Auxerre when Alan Hill put the local newspaper in front of me. The headline read something like: "Forest have a fat goalkeeper who is very slow and we can exploit this."

I was supposed to be the weak link, fat, cumbersome and leaden-footed. Whoever wrote that couldn't have seen me for two years because, apart from the clanger I made against Bolton, I had hardly made a mistake. It spurred me on and I got man of the match as we won 1-0, so that rammed their headline right back down their throats. I managed to save a shot from Moussa Saib with my legs and tipped away a shot from Stephane Guivarc'h as we drew 0-0 at the City Ground.

We drew Olympique Lyonnais in the next round, another big name. We pipped them 1-0 at the City Ground with a goal from Paul McGregor, who tapped in a rebound from Pearcey's penalt. We then drew 0-0 at their place, after defending superby under pressure for 90 minutes. The Forest fans were magnificent that night; the atmosphere was unreal.

Next up the mighty Bayern Munich in the quarter-finals. We went to Bayern and had another fantastic game in front of a crowd of 38,000 in the Olympic Stadium. We lost 2-1, but at least we had the luxury of an away goal from Steve Chettle. Chetts was Mr Reliable. I hadn't seen him for about 12 years until we played in a charity game together recently and he hadn't changed a bit – apart from a few grey hairs.

In the return at the City Ground, we went at them for half and hour and they were clearing balls off the line and we were hitting post and bar. Then they got a free-kick outside the box and Christian Ziege curled the ball under the wall and it slipped under my body and into the net. It was the first real save I had to make, but I had a slight lack of concentration and the ball ended up in the net. As soon as they scored their second we had to chase the game and you can't do that against a quality side like Bayern. We ended up losing 5-1 with a consolation goal from Steve Stone, but it had been a great journey and we had a fantastic time. Let's face it, it was a great achievement for a small squad like ours to get that far.

Towards the end of the season we got thumped 5-0 at Old Trafford. I didn't have a bad game, the simple fact was they murdered us. But Frank Clark wasn't happy, to say the least. He kicked the dressing-room door which bounced back and hit him in the face. He went round every player in turn, having a go, face as red as a beetroot. He said:

"Des Lyttle what position do you play?"

"Right-back boss."

"Well fucking play right-back then."

"Do you realise who you are playing against?"

"Ryan Giggs boss."

"You are overlapping and can't get back because your arse is too big. Just play right-back."

"Bart-Williams, you gave a penalty away. Stay on your feet you idiot. He was going away from goal."

Just then he suddenly spun round and pointed at fitness coach Graham Lyas, who was sat with his feet on the table. It made him jump and he fell off his chair. I looked round and Des Lyttle had a towel over his face mopping up the tears, he was laughing that much. It was no laughing matter, losing 5-0, of course, but it was strange to see someone who was normally so placid lose it big style like that.

In 1996 I was linked with a move to Leeds. They offered two and a half million for me, which was accepted by Forest. The Forest chairman, Fred Reacher, said he didn't want me to go. They could have done with the money at the time, but he said he would leave it with me. I always undervalued myself and I was flattered by the big price tag so I went up for talks with the manager, Howard Wilkinson. Leeds had signed Ian Rush earlier in the day and the place was going mad so they had to sneak me in through the back door to avoid the press. What they offered me was amazing – a four-year contract worth £300,000 a year and £2,000 per game appearance money.

Marseille were also said to be interested and if I had gone I would have been the first Englishman to leave on a Bosman. I could have made a fortune by going to Marseille or Leeds, but I was settled at Forest. My friends were all there. I respected the boss and I think he respected me.

This was never really about money. At the end of the day, I just wanted to be happy. I really don't know what all the fuss was about. I just wanted to find out what I was worth. That's what freedom of contract is all about.

I had been at the City Ground for eight years and I wanted to stay there until the end of my career. Honestly, I just wanted to wait until the end of the season when there was more time and fewer distractions, so we could sit down and sort it out.

In the end I signed a contract which almost doubled my money. But it was a lot less than I would have got at Leeds so I don't think anyone can accuse me of being a money grabber, can they?

When I moved to Sherwood I rented a bedroom downstairs from a chap called Brendan Wheat, who worked as a doorman at a bar in Nottingham called Browns, which was one of Roy Keane's favourite haunts. I think Brendan, who was mates with Gary Charles, even threw Roy out of Browns a couple of times! I eventually bought the house from Brendan, who had the Olympic Health & Fitness club in Nottingham, before he moved to Marbella.

I used to have an African grey parrot. I'd had the decorators in for a week and one night I sat watching TV when I heard "Forest are wankers." I didn't know where it was coming from until the parrot said it again. The decorators had obviously nobbled it and I ended up giving it to Brendan for his gym.

One day I was woken by a noise upstairs. I knew Brendan was away so I picked up a snooker cue and went upstairs to find a youth climbing out of the window. I'd been burgled. I ran downstairs and chased him down the drive, but he managed to vault the security gate before I could catch him. It was probably just as well, as I was stark naked and wielding a snooker cue. God knows what the police would have made of that one!

There used to be an intercom on the gates and it was a nightmare when it came time for the kids to leave school. They would press the button and shout obscenities at me.

Apart from that, I enjoyed living in Sherwood and my daughter, Lilli, was born there. But I have to say l have never been happier than when I lived in a quiet little cul-de-sac in Edwalton. It was so quiet and we hardly saw anyone apart from the neighbours. I used to love playing for the local cricket club during the summer and, to be honest, I never wanted to leave.

One night in Ginza, a Japanese restaurant which was our favourite haunt in Sherwood, I invented a new delicacy, char-grilled Crossley. There were eight of us round the table, Colin Cooper, Ian Woan, Kevin Campbell and our partners.

Being regulars, the owners used to let us go behind the counter to do a party trick. The idea was that you had to flick an egg up and catch it in the chef's hat without breaking the shell. I failed miserably with my first attempt, but persuaded them to let me have another go.

Unfortunately, this time I lost my balance and lurched forward towards the 800 degree sizzling hot plate. Fortunately, I managed to put my knuckles down first instead of the palms of my hands. I was stuck to the metal and they had to peel me off. The pain was unbelievable, but they were obviously used to dealing with clumsy prats like me and put some cooling powder on the burns straight away. Some Sake helped kill the pain and I didn't even have to go to hospital. But my knuckles were red raw and I was off work for a about a week.

But that wasn't the worst trouble I landed myself in. That happened on a trip to America when I almost drowned Craig Armstrong. When we won promotion back to the Premier League we were told we could pick any destination in the world for a ten-day end-of-season trip.

We chose Miami. Better still there were no gaffers on the trip, just coach Steve Beaglehole. One day we decided it would be a good idea to hire a boat, load it with booze and explore the waterways of Florida. We were chugging along but it got a bit boring and I decided to liven things up by going out to sea, ignoring the 'No Admittance' and 'Danger' signs along the way.

It was OK at first but then it started to get a bit choppy and waves started coming over the front of the little boat, which was obviously not sea-worthy. I don't know if it was the weight of the booze or fat lads like me, but we suddenly started to go down like the Titanic, 600 yards out to sea.

Unfortunately, Craig Armstrong, at the back of the boat, couldn't swim and Dave Beasant had to grab him round the neck and life-save him safely back to shore. We were busy collecting the floating flip-flops and beer cans that were being washed up on the shore when we heard the sound of sirens in the distance so we legged it. Unfortunately, we had done a lot of damage to the boat. The insurance covered most of it, but we all had to chip in the pay for the rest.

Season 1996-97 was certainly one to forget. It was a disaster. Forest were relegated from the Premier League after finishing rock bottom with just six wins, five points behind Middlesbrough. And 'Boro had three points deducted at that! Things were so bad that Alfie Haaland was joint top scorer in the League with six goals, after Kevin Campbell was sidelined through injury.

Frank Clark quit and Stuart Pearce was given the job as player-manager. He managed to conjure up five wins in a row to get the 'Manager of the Month' award but, ultimately, even he couldn't save this sinking club and left for pastures new at New-castle at the end of the season. Forest paid a club record £3,500,000 to Celtic for Pierre van Hooijdonk after a loan spell, while Dean Saunders finally arrived at the club from Galatasaray.

We had a low-key pre-season, apart from friendlies with Chelsea and Manchester United, but we made a flying start with a 3-0 win at Coventry, Kevin Campbell weighing in with his first hat-trick for the club. Then we lost 4-1 at home to Sunderland. They only had six shots on target, but scored four goals, while we had 15 shots off target.

Dean Saunders scored his first League goal for the club in the 2-2 draw at Southampton, but we lost 4-1 at Manchester United as we went 16 League games without a win.

We lost 4-2 at Liverpool and Stan Collymore typically got two. Robbie Fowler also scored and Des Lyttle conceded an own goal after 51 minutes. I loved playing at Anfield. The fans were something special. Most clubs gave visiting goalkeepers a lot of stick, but the Kop used to clap you into goal. Everton fans are the same.

We finally broke the losing habit by beating Arsenal 2-1 at the City Ground with two from Alfie Haaland, but then lost 4-0 at home to Manchester United. It was a freezing night and we caught a cold as David Beckham and Nicky Butt scored in the first half, Solskjaer and Andy Cole after the break. Beckham did me with a chip from an angle right into the far corner.

Andy Cole was brilliant. I played with him at Fulham and although he took some stick from the critics, his finishing was frightening. He was some player. Two days later we drew 2-2 at Leicester. It was freezing again, but over 20,000 still turned up. Emile Heskey and Muzzy Izzet scored for Leicester, Nigel Clough and Colin Cooper, three minutes from time, for us.

On New Year's Day we won 1-0 at West Ham thanks to a

37th-minute goal from Kevin Campbell and we followed that up with five in a row against Ipswich and Newcastle in the FA Cup and West Ham (1-0), Chelsea (2-0) and Spurs (2-1) in the League. Then things started to go wrong and we went 11 games without a win, including four successive 1-1 draws.

Pearcey's passion carried us along for a while, but we reached a new low when we lost 1-0 at Division Two Chesterfield in the FA Cup. And we were lucky to get nil, we were that bad!

Even though we were not playing that well in the league at the time, we thought we just had to turn up to win. But we showed no passion or desire.

We thought the place was a shithole and had the wrong attitude. We were simply shocking and let everyone down. To make matters worse, I got sent off by referee David Elleray after conceding a penalty which Tom Curtis converted, Chesterfield fans still remind me about that match to this day.

Caretaker-boss Stuart Pearce wasn't happy to say the least, but he didn't blame me. But some supporters did. I was talking to my dad outside the ground when two or three of them started to have a go at me and I had to be dragged back inside before there was trouble. At the end of the season I needed a hernia operation. I had been playing with it for a month and Forest had been keeping it secret with Tommy Wright on loan at Reading. I was only training one day a week and ended up with a double hernia. It finally went on me in the game at Southampton and Alan Fettis came in for the last four games.

I wish I had gone in for the operation sooner because I would certainly have ended up playing more football. To make matter worse, there was uncertainty off the pitch, with the club up for sale. Van Hooijdonk made his debut in the 1-1 draw against Blackburn, but he managed only one goal in his eight games, making some wonder if he could hack it at this level.

You can't save them all....

It's Christmas party time with Des Lyttle

Sitting watching on the sidelines was driving me mad

CHAPTER EIGHT

Under Pressure Again

I was under pressure at the City Ground after Dave Bassett took over as manager. His brief was to get the club promoted again and he certainly delivered the goods as Forest stormed to the Division One title.

I liked Bassett, even though I never played under him. Jason Lee, Bryan Roy and Alfie Inge Haaland all departed and Bassett brought in Andy Johnson, Alan Rogers, Geoff Thomas and Thierry Bonalair. There was talk that the club was signing Kevin Miller from Watford on a five-year deal as competition for me and Alan Fettis, who was on the transfer list.

In the end Miller went to Palace instead. So Bassett signed Marco Pascolo, the Swiss No.1, from Cagliari for £750,000, but he wasn't the best. I was struggling with a back injury which flared up on the pre-season trip to Finland so Pascolo went straight into the side, although he only played five games before Dave Beasant came in on loan and took over.

My back was so bad at this stage that I had trouble tying my shoe laces. The only cure was rest and I was out for almost a year. It was breaking my heart and having to sit it out so long was a nightmare.

There was apparently a bulge in a disc which was catching a nerve, but I was adamant I was not having another operation. The only good point was that it allowed me to spend time with my daughter Lilli. It was a good job I wasn't playing because it was exhausting being a father. Football-wise, that year had been one of the worst of my life. I was depressed and I had been arguing with my wife, Gaynor, but more of that later.

Bryan Roy moved to Germany for £1.5m and Clough, Haaland, Pearce and Saunders had all gone. So you wouldn't have bet much on Forest winning the league that season. But they did.

They lost only eight league games, scoring 82 goals and conceding only 42 in 46 games. Pierre van Hooijdonk bagged 34 goals in total, while Kevin Campbell got 23. I think Colin Cooper was the next best with five, so you can see that it was a tremendous contribution by the two strikers.

I have to say that Pierre was one of the best strikers of a dead ball I have ever seen. He perhaps didn't hit it as hard as Pearcey, but he was more accurate and technical.

The departing players had left a big hole, quality-wise, but Jon Olav Hjelde arrived along with Christan Edwards. Jon didn't say much when he first arrived at the City Ground, but he turned out to be a great guy. He was prone to injury, but he was a real force in the air.

I owe him one because he got a load of electronic gear imported into England for me. And it was top-of-the-range stuff, Bang & Olufsen, no rubbish. It should have cost £25k, but he got if for me for £8k. It was top quality, in fact I've only just got rid of the television. Jon, Lars Bohinen and Alfie Inge Haaland were also great to have along on pre-season trips to Norway and Sweden, because they knew the best places to visit.

At least Wales had not forgotten me and in January 1997 Bobby Gould rang me out of the blue. But I was now competing against Paul Jones (Southampton), former Forest 'keeper Andy Marriott and Darren Ward (Notts County).

I was back in training in November, but I was now No.3 in the pecking order, so I needed to go out on loan to get a game. In the end Billy Bonds came in to take me on loan to Millwall.

I had been training hard and had played one game for the reserves, but there is no substitute for regular first-team football, so off I went.

Millwall certainly wouldn't have been my first choice. It's an intimidating place to visit and I must admit that I didn't want to go. I wanted to play somewhere closer to home.

But I desperately needed first-team action and, to be fair, they were the only ones who had asked.

I only arrived at The Den an hour before kick-off in the home game against Northampton, so there wasn't much time for introductions, but I managed to keep a clean sheet. We drew 1-1 with Watford and Oldham but then lost 1-0 at Carlisle.

I was suddenly enjoying myself again and we pipped Gillingham 1-0 in front of a crowd of 8,241. Goals from Shaw and Gray gave us a 2-1 win at Fulham, but we lost 1-0 to both Wrexham and Preston and 3-1 at Chesterfield.

We beat Chris Waddle's Burnley 1-0 and managed a 1-1 draw at home to Bristol Rovers, but my thirteen-game loan spell ended with a 2-0 defeat at Walsall and a 1-1 draw at home to Plymouth, before Nigel Spink came back.

It was a bit of a culture shock after the City Ground, I must admit. The football was a bit more basic than I was used to with a lot of high balls and physical play. Millwall didn't have much of a side then, but I enjoyed the experience.

The boss, Billy Bonds, was great. He let me train in Nottingham to cut down on travelling and I ended up playing 13 League games for them.

They had Kenny Brown, Andy Gray (ex-Palace not the ex-Sky Andy Gray) and a young Lucas Neil, but that was about it. Gray was a lad. We used to travel to games in style, on the England team bus no less. One day I went to get on the bus and there were a load of irons and kettles where the skips normally go, Andy was trying to flog them to the lads. It took me back to my early days at Forest when I used to take slippers in to sell at Christmas.

The club put me up in a luxury hotel on Canary Wharf, which was nice, and I started to feel at home until Billy telephoned and told me to get a taxi to the ground. Apparently some fans weren't happy with the way the team was playing and were wrecking the players' cars. Like I said, it was a bit of a culture shock.....

In 1998-99, Forest beat Coventry and Southampton but then went a club record 19 games without a win. Big Ron Atkinson came in for the last few games of the season, but had no chance of saving us from relegation really. He hit the headlines, as usual, when he went to the wrong dugout for his first game against Arsenal.

But I liked Big Ron and Forest could have done worse than give him the job full time. If they had, I might never have ended up leaving the City Ground.

Jean-Claude Darcheville was quick, but only scored twice in 16 games. He was still coming to terms with the death of his wife and children in a car accident. He could play a bit and certainly did well in France and in his spell with Rangers.

Pearcey was back at the City Ground with West Ham as we drew 0-0, but we lost 4-0 to Coventry. Darren Huckerby, who might have been a Forest player, bagged a hat-trick. A goal from Pierre Van Hooijdonk gave us a rare 1-0 win at Everton, but our fate was sealed when we won only one of the next 12 games.

That included a record 8-1 home hammering by champions Manchester United. It was only 2-1 at the break, but we were sunk by super sub Solskjaer, who scored four in ten minutes.

Before the game Big Ron put the United team up on his famous flip-chart and told us not to worry about Jesper Blomqvist because he was "ordinary."

Now this guy cost United £4.4m and played in the 1994 World Cup with Sweden. He was so average that he set up six of the goals. Typically, after the game Ron, the master of one liners, said: "See, I told you he was average!"

Boy, was I glad I wasn't playing in that game. Nevertheless, I was itching to get back and told Ron that I was ready.

I shared the goalkeeping duties with Dave Beasant, who was left out at Charlton after leaking 13 goals in three games. I only knew at 12.45pm that I would be playing. It was a bit like when I made my first team debut all those years before.

It was typical of Dave Beasant that he came and wished me well before the game. I was nervous in the dressing room because I hadn't played in the Premiership for 22 months.

I had been sent out on loan at Millwall and had been replaced by a 40-year-old so the prospects for the future didn't look good, did they?

There are easier games to make your comeback in than Charlton but, when you play in the Premiership, there are no easy games. It was just great to be back and I got the man-of-the-match reviews after saving a penalty. After 68 minutes Steve Chettle brought down John Robinson and referee Stephen Lodge pointed straight to the spot.

Fortunately, Neil Redfearn hit the spot-kick quite close to me. I also saved a penalty from Benny Carbone against Sheffield Wednesday and we managed to beat fellow strugglers Blackburn, for once, with goals from Dougie Freedman and Chris Bart-Williams.

In the end we finished rock bottom. But who knows what might have happened had Pierre not gone on his one-man crusade over the sales of Colin Cooper and Kevin Campbell?

Pierre had a point. But he should have just got on with his job, scoring goals. He should have concentrated on doing his best for the team and then leave at the end of the season if he still wasn't happy.

He ended up playing 19 games and scored six goals. So, maybe, he couldn't cut it in the Premier League after all?

The Forest squad under Dave Bassett

The only consolation about being injured was that it left me with more time to spend with my daughter Lilli

Celebrating with Kevin Campbell, who scored a hat-trick against Coventry

David Platt's Forest squad

New boss David Platt reveals his three 'big' Italian signings

CHAPTER NINE
The Italian Job

Former England star David Platt replaced big Ron Atkinson and immediately brought three Italians in with him. They didn't play much, but they were great cooks bless them. They made superb pasta. I give them credit for that.

Moreno Mannini at least had a bit of pedigree and had been capped ten times by Italy. He had won the Serie A title with Sampdoria and played in the 1992 European Cup final against Barcelona at Wembley. The other two, right-winger Gianluca Petrachi and Salvatore Matrecano, cost the club £4.8m. What a monumental waste of money that was....

Petrachi made just 12 appearances before he was sent back to Perugia on a season-long loan, while Matrecano made just two appearances in the League Cup. Mannini played eight times before he too disappeared into the wilderness.

There were rumours that the players made them outcasts at the club, but that simply wasn't true. The trouble was they didn't seem to be match fit and couldn't get to grips with the English game.

But I must admit, I did like to wind the Italian lads up. They thought belching and farting were in bad taste, so I would sit on the toilet with the door open, reading a newspaper, shout them over and ambush them.

We had been playing the likes of Manchester United, Chelsea, Spurs and Liverpool. Now we were travelling to places like Grimsby, Walsall, Port Vale, Crewe and Tranmere.

John Terry came in on loan to Forest from Chelsea as a youngster. He only played five games but you could see, even then, that he had the makings of a future England captain.

It was a big year for me with my testimonial coming along. I had just turned 30 and the next contract was probably the most important of my career. I wanted a five-year deal, to see out the rest of my career at Forest. I wanted something sorted, especially with Dave Beasant back at the club on a one-year deal.

But injury struck again just 18 minutes into the Worthington Cup tie at Bristol City. I did ankle ligaments in the 0-0 draw, but fortunately we went through 2-1 on aggregate. It happened when I collided with the post and fell badly after tipping away a chip from Craig Goodridge. We produced some good displays, but were weren't good enough to get promoted.

We finished 14th in Division One, which was about right. Goals had again been a problem with Van Hooijdonk, Shipperley, Stone and Darcheville all gone and Dougie Freedman and Alan Rogers bagging nine in the league. I ended up playing 20 League games. The final one was the 1-1 draw at QPR in January.

A lady called Dianne Brown launched the campaign to keep me at the City Ground. It was signed by hundreds of fans. I can't tell you how humble that made me feel. At least someone wanted me!

It had been all over the papers that it looked as though my days were numbered. I did not want to go, but David Platt was making it impossible for me to stay. Then Dianne came up with the idea for a petition and I was touched that so many fans cared about my future. I was honoured that so many fans took the trouble to sign a petition.

During the game against QPR in January I took off my jersey to reveal a T-shirt which read 'No Matter What Happens To Me I Will Always Love You The Supporters At NFFC'.

I had been at the club for ten years and feared this might be the last chance to say a proper farewell to the Forest fans. I'd seen one or two players do a similar thing in the past.

During the game, bearing in mind I hadn't played in the first team for a while, the fans were brilliant to me. They cheered me at every opportunity. After the game I threw my top to a fan in the crowd.

What I said on the shirt then still holds true to this day! I'm still a follower and a supporter, even now. I still look for Forest's result every Saturday night.

The trouble was, I knew, deep down, that it was going to be my last game for the club. And I just wanted to let the fans know how much I appreciated their support.

I thought "Sod it I'm going for it." I heard later that David Platt wasn't happy about it, but he never said anything to me. Not that I blame him.

Looking back it was probably a stupid thing to do. If one of my players did that now, I would be upset.

But I had made my mind up that I was going to do it and that's that. I even went to the toilets to put it on under my shirt because I didn't want any of the players, and especially the staff, to see what I was up to. The main thing is, that the crowd appreciated the gesture.

Now, I want to take this opportunity to say a personal 'Thank You' to all the fans who supported me. Unfortunately, there were a lot of names that I couldn't read. The handwriting was worse than mine, and that's saying something....

The Petition From Many Of
The Fans That Support

Nottingham Forest

Who Wish To Keep

Mark Crossley

Playing Where They Think He
Belongs.

At

The City Ground

May 8th 2000

Elaine Reid	J Stringer	B Stevenson
Stephen Crosswell	L Spencer	K Stevenson
J Eyson	Neil Harrison	D Mason
J Eyson	Paul Crookes	J Scott
K Hardy	C Bartram	Dale Martin
K Butler	L Bartram	J Spurgin
P Coates	L Butcher	P Whitby
G Cheetham	L Wright	L Elliott
P Taylor	P Beresford	J Gregory
S Taylor	R Beresford	Paul Lane
I Julian	C Pundel	Pete Harris
G Hough	KW Marshall	C Tinsley
P Squires	M Clements	Rachel Derry
L Shooter	C Keen	JR Bradwate
M Shooter	MD Wright	Paul Allsop
G Eggleston	M Fidler	David Poole
M Pope	D Fidler	Dave Harlow
C Cooke	S Singleton	Michael Rayns
B Austen	J Turner	C Flint
M Austen	C Highton	H Law
J Wallhead	J Crudgington	P Suggins
Jo Wallhead	D Cox	Danny Crate
LA Wright	S Cox	I Hamed
Lee R Wright	G Burton	Tracey Cuttell
David Wright	P Davies	D West
Aleks Gajic	L Dawson	J Roberts
Martin Allen	A Dawson	J Scott
H Foster	S Dawson	T Bradshaw
S Truman	AJ Ostler	P Smith
AB Cutts	DJ Ostler	E Wright
B Forster	M Buckley	Nigel Owen
P Lawton	D Buckley	Ricky Marshall
JW Maddison	C Morrell	V Marshall
Angela Vickers	R Morrell	Patricia Warner
Joanne Thompson	A Morrell	Sandra Oswin
Carl Thomson	P Nicholas	Colin Oswin
Vikki Foster	T Hardy	Eileen Bowen
Tim James	S Meacock	Chris Blaydon
Sean Revill	B Walkden	Rodney Wray
R Rolston	P Cherry	I Brown
M Ashley	SW Hall	Mandy Stuart
J Garner	Steve Spence	F Cousins
G Radford	A Wilkinson	R Fearon
G Caldwell	J Iqbal	T James
A Musson	P Saward	J Larkson
D Musson	G Clarkson	P Roscoe
R Smithson	S Phillips	A Smith
AP Musson	DA Smith	Mark Lord
A Barlow	L Cowling	MW Cunnington
RA Jenkins	S Crowston	Mark James
Claire Morrison	S Nevin	S Collins
K Morrison	P Penera	K Wood

G Johnstone	C Parker	M Orange
L Mendleson	D Smith	S Beecher
Rona Julien	R Bartles	C Warwick
Mike West	S Martin	E Warwick
P Oakenfield	P Ball	CH Warwick
Philip Moult	R Hull	G Payne
Jane Dale	C Armstrong	S Payne
M Dillon	D Binch	Mrs Troke
R Mallard	E Forman	J Collinson
Wayne Smith	H Fisher	J Naisbett
Z Rafique	B Fisher	P Revill
M Coals	A Lees	K Miles
Russell Coney	S Farmer	RJ More
Sam Marquee	H Clarke	A Lee
F Mohamed	R Haywood	David Mee
A Flowers	P Brett	S Hill
T Ford	S Beeby	Laura Griffin
S Payne	D Cox	P Wilks
K Morris	K Murphy	C Marson
Steve Cummings	T Murphy	C Ashmore
H Wright	G Lee	E Ashmore
Kyle Youens	K Maybin	H Muster
R Wilson	A Jennings	A Green
E Cartwright	J Scott	A Taylor
J Clough	J Bourne	C Swales
Ian Westbury	P Bourne	A Worrall
Frank Whitt	S Boulton	V Carney
Andrew Cowling	M Tolly	T Green
P Moore	J Brown	D Hanson
J Buckingham	W Smalley	J Hanson
S Roberts	D Marshall	L Stevens
M Masser	K Askham	Dawn Coe
Paul Taylor	J Cross	A Guest
T Pearce	M Cross	S Marlowe
Martin Smalley	Amy Rhoades	Lynn Hunter
Joanne Fitch	C Hindson	S Fenton
Paul Cobb	Keith Goodson	R Read
JH Lymbury	Thomas Goodson	AF Doran
M Pritchard	Cherry Goodson	M Day
O Cooper	Joan Radshaw	J Weston
B Sykes	Tracey Tatlow	M Hawley
E Warwick	Richard Tatlow	F Rice
Diane Brown	Tara Tatlow	C Rice
Russell Brown	GR Taylor	A Maynard
M Warwick	A Slade	S Maynard
A Wright	K Purkin	D Lanyon
M.T. Wright	M Trewsdale	S Lanyon
Jim Brown	M Dirkin	D Taylor
Simon Pearce	G Christie	M Bradley
Adam Perczynshi	C Ghent	Matt Storey
L Smith	P Harrison	Troy Mallard
P Neal	G Orange	Dean Longdon

SK Smith
D Searles
K Yeates
Tom Staszkiewicz
Joe Staszkiewicz
Lloyd Staszkiewicz
Diane Hill
Ian Pollard
L Geehan
J Geehan
K Geehan
T Cooke
R Woodward
Andrew Fraser
Fred Walker
Colin Allan
Matt Dobson
Glenn Barker
Carl Barker
David Colclough
Sarah Barthorpe
Val Northage
Louise Northage
Dominic Reilly
Joseph Reilly
S Baldwin
C Clarke
J Brown
R Mather
P Newton
S Jackson
K Jackson
E Etherington
A Pont
S Pont
Sarah O'Carroll
E Elvidge
G Lomax
M Mellors
MA Mellors
D Waterall
N Simpson
M Colyer
D King
R Clarke
A Marks
P Marks
T Sharpe
D Rigley
S Bridge
L Challans
K Ottewell

A Ottewell
D Bell
S Bell
K Bell
A Birch
A Elliott
C Elliott
P Hallam
M Lane
S Day
K Bond
C Cummins
A Pinkett
S Gilpin
J Horsley
K Horsley
N Reeve-Jones
T Congreve
Alex Davis
Steve Hopewell
Lee Wilcockson
Ady Curtis
Mark Emmerson
Mark Lenton
Darren Curtis
Daren Marrison
Liz Sowter
Cath Sowter
Andrew Edwards
Wendy Coxon
Rob Palethorpe
D Palethorpe
Alan Fowler
Gina Redfern
Anthony Moore
Craig Moore
Steve Moore
Louisa Scoggins
David Scoggins
Pat O'Hara
Shane O'Hare
Des Oldham
Barnaby Pritchard
Paul Abbiss
David Abbiss
Michael Rayns
Christine Ross
Anthea Hannah
Paul Barnett
Peter Rinkert
C Shaw
D Shaw

D Watson
J Baldwin
J Middup
W Middup
R Middup
C Sargeant
W Lovegrove
Steve Lakin
E Redgate
L Davenport
R Sanderson
Alan Davis
Gareth Waplington
Lee Deller
Nicola Haddon
Rosano Leto
Kelly Fowler
Ben Crosby
Craig Taylor
Michael Slater
Sheila Phillips
Claire Phillips
Paula Dent
Dean Minett
A Holland
M Crick
Steve Phillips
Simon Vickers
J Evans
J Riley
K Holland
G Riley
W Trevillion
D Burns
SJ Burns
C Parr
A Turner
C Dale
A Dale
Alan Smit
Graham Smit
Mike Price
Nicky Price
Andrew Walker
Penny Walker
G Haywood
T Key
R Carroll
Craig Watson
C Charlton
E Kemp
H Baldwin

Scott Marshall	D Swinton	J Ahsmole
R Marshall	M Kilcline	Amanda Brooks
C Cooper	P Thompson	A Smith
D Emery	Jimmy Tobin	M Duriez
A Emery	L Dyer	Mandy Buck
R Emery	C Drake	Shiela Gordon
T Marsden	N Smith	F Hudson
S Wilderspin	J Viola	S Green
M Winfield	AB Melnyk	P Frost
H Winfield	A Melnyk	D Hammond
D Underhill	K Melnyk	Kelly Cassidy
J Underhill	S Bayliss	Eddie Watt
S Fowler	K Brown	Judy Webster
D Brown	T Burton	Ian Sayers
T Bunston	M Phillips	Asa Ostling
L Sides	K Morrison	Nick Brazener
A Reid	K Lievesley	Chris Milburn
S Reid	J Fox	Sue Rowburger
K Hibbett	J Waheed	Tomny Hiorns
R Smith	S Litchfield	James Lievesley
P Smith	C Brookes	David Pegg
D Smith	R Lee	David Nicol
S Lumby	J Lee	Andrew Turner
J Thurgood	S Lee	Kelly Warwick
N Brookes	S Beresford	Alan Sims
A Roe	R Towson	Michael Rayns
P Summers	S Jones	Heather Rayns
A Harrington	K Hill	Sarah Oldknow
GaryWard	A Robinson	Seb Thomas
Neil Griffin	D Zimsek	Neil Harrison
John Hill	S Keeling	Steve Hill
L Bower	E Keen	P Steven
K Miller	J Gordon	B Thornhill
C Miller	Jamie Cox	M Poole
R Miller	Lee Cox	M Foster
S Marson	Dean Asher	J Simpson
C Smith	David Barker	J Warwick
L Charlesworth	Lee Richardson	CAJ Warwick
Ian Wright	I Glover	M Glenn
P Smith	Adam Priest	T Stewart
J Webster	Mark Hutchinson	A Mullins
Carl Cox	Daniel Tarr	A Tatlow
Gary Chantler	P Bolton	Adam Tatlow
Andrew Cannon	J Carney	Carol Green
S Warburton	J Potter	Danny Brown
J Parkinson	John Priest	W Brown
C Norman	H Morley	J Warwick
C Williams	M Twigger	J Forest
D O'Brien	R Upton	N West
M Bolton	R Flowers	N Wales
P Dainty	G Cargg	G Bignall
C Underhill	Debra Robinson	J Younger

M Pink
A Brown
I Crosby
A Ryan
M Duff
A Wakefield
K Stevens
S Lovegrove
E Chivers
S Chivers
S Fitzgerald
D Colclough
G Haywood
M Marriott
C Oakly
C Jackson
S Jackson
B Gibson
J Mercer
G Smith
J Straw
Jackie Straw
G Breward
Liz Cooper
M Meal
D Padgington
Scott Hedley
S Desai
M Martin
S Graham
D Hopewell
R Mayor
A Norton
R Smith
T Harrison
S Sandor
R Boultby
A Percival
S Cross
M Garner
A Mason
M Rose
C Garner
B Clarke
R Clarke
Dawn Clarke
O Pearce
M Winfield
W Winfield
K Newton
John Cooper
Gill Gamston

Martin Smith
Roy Radford
RJ Stanley
Robert Radford
Richard Radford
Neil Gough
A Doran
R Truman
C Boot
M Smith
J Reilly
G Taylor
A Dixon
R Paling
N Paling
M Hind
M Bullock
J Bullock
A Brooks
L Bexon
A Saxton
K Burnham
D Pell
R Pennacchia
L Pennacchia
P Poole
P Hardy
P Howe
A Howe
C Quick
S Hammonds
B Martin
J Martin
G Berry
A Davis
M Shaw
K Camm
M Camm
N Curtis
M Walls
G Daniels
J Crutchlow
K Tolan
A Cooper
A Huszarik
C Glen
K Dilks
M Ball
N Brown
D Astill
J Brown
Hilary Davies

A Gill
B Fox
K Fox
P Worrall
C Brine
D Stevens
M Vaughan
A Sanders
Sue Brant
D Fitzgerald
E Burgin
T Ashley
D Mitchinson
D Bolton
P Boddy
A Fox
R West
B West
J West
R Harris
Y Key
C Nix
M Nix
Ian Butler
D Hallott
Jane Coates
Trevor Parr
Darren Fee
Neil Hogan
David Earl
LW Shaw
M Shaw
Ray Pope
D Bartram
D Badder
M Badder
A Grey
R Wrigjht
M Wright
T Lomax
M Fisher
E Turner
JB Smith
P Edgington
S Rigby
B Garner
Sharon Cullingan
MD Clark
J Finnigan
D Lawrence
R Berkly
B Lewis

133

R Page
M Page
G Wells
A Wells
Mark Waterall
Craig Ashington
L Dawson
M Williams
Ben Wilde
Paul Markham
Linda Markham
Susan Markham
Richard Markham
N Coverdale
Claire Helstrip
Louise Abrahams
John DiMarco
M Brookes
M Wall
M Bartlett
D Hickman
P Espley
S McQueen
Rob Blackwell
J Scrivens
P Hancock
V Wright
M Booth
W Rogers
M Doran
R Hoy
J Fowler
R Fowler
G Leman
D Grainger
S Paling
S Lee
J Binch
M Aldridge
E Blackhall
C Ball
Heather King
L Bryan
I Hobby
I Phillips
R Dyer
S Hogg
R Brown
K Lumb
C Kingsland
T Pikett
J George

M Davies
D Davies
G Davies
A Crosby
C Wilmot
J Wilmot
J Bamford
S Bannister
A Shaw
L Marks
P Garry
C Henson
D Hudson
R Hudson
J Bown
D Lee
B Cantrill
J Smith
I Briggs
R Briggs
M Ferrelly
T Ferrelly
L Wilson
C Gough
C Jarvis
A O'Brien
H Pickup
D Shandham
I Deakin
S Baker
P Marshall
S Lloyd
J Wood
B Curtain
S Curtain
M Scloney
C Scolney
Craig Scolney
M Singleton
C Wilson
K Bennett
Lee Bennett
A Williams
C Tynan
L Ellis
Ian Hill
Gavin Ellis
Wendy Pearson
D Brown
R Brown
G Stocks
S King

K Bott
P Brown
L Brown
D Harrison
E Cousins
H Cousins
T Tatlow
Pat Brown
Ken Brown
M Smith
S Barnett
M Moore
G Anderws
D Crossley
J Simms
I Cheetham
W Burkes
M Orange
D Phillips
J Coggin
I Coggin
Iris White
A Hurst
Phil Marsh
Kim Lehouckia
S Clarke
T Broughton
A Kanabar
J Harris
Sam Gray
Tony Marks
M Warnock
M Leivers
J Dobson
L Coupland
T Lees
D Pykett
N Randle
C Wycks
W Wycks
E Mayfield
P Kirchin
S Fowler
D Henson
JB Henson
K Hemsley
C Hemsley
J Teece
W Teece
D Lacey
N Lacey
P Locker

D Challans
A Gillott
R Carrington
D Booth
J Meakin
M Hancock
S Smith
D Toplis
R Staszkiewicz
R Davies
K Walters
S Carr
E Holmes
P Turton
C Holmes
P O'Kane
D Burton
P Stevenson
K Braithwaite
S Hornbuckle
J Sharpe
A Jones
S Thompson
R Bridge
M England
K England
P Hearne
T Hearne
S Jones
D Nunn
K Perry
J Perry
Andy Williams
Chris Williams
A Riley
Marilyn Crossley
Michael Crossley
B Clayton
B Clarke
M Brown
L Bradley
Steve Lane
Ron Shilton
Neal Hammersley
Daniel Tonks
Martin Burton
Michael Page
C McBride
C Orme
S Harlow
A Shephard
J Pearce

D Pearce
T Sinclair
M Rudd
I Harvey
D Rowe
Mark Harmsen
Roger Claricoats
Gary Andrews
A Roe
Jane Whitehead
Diane Whitehead
Brian Cumberpatch
Matt Turner
Rich Hale
Steve Bentley
Paul Richardson
Philip Woods
Adam Shinfield
Craig Shaw
Simon Wall
John Soar
Tyson Stacey
Eric Griffiths
S Dury
B Timson
J Kund
C Lord
R Brentnall
M Palfrey
W Ellis
M Howard
L Manterfield
G Davies
K Roberts
Jenny Taylor
M Freer
E Smith
A Smith
C Barker
C Greasley
W McFarlane
S Sheppard
R McLean
G Austin
M Duncan
D Tassi
S Tassi
M George
K Greenhalgh
D Jepson
C Palfrey
J Butler

H Statham
A Terry
D Cheeseman
P Gatehouse
K Timson
G Freer
L Thomas
Ray Thomas
J McLean
M McLean
D Shaw
S Palling
P Sanderson
Reg Atkins
Gerald Atkins
Phil Turner
Alan Rose
Neil Briggs
Wendy Waites
John Smith
Sue Price
Chris Price
P Gee
P Dawson
R Harper
C Harper
D Feely
L Dean
B Huckerby
M Marsh
D Brown
Dave McLean
A Howard
R Beech
D Hume
S West
J Pack
Dave Ingham
Jayne Gray
D Shanahan
P Sykes
D Sykes
M Turner
G Turner
D Hufton
S Hufton
R Cosmor
L Cosmor
A Lightly
P Lightly
N Ward

My farewell message to the magnificent Nottingham Forest fans at QPR

An advert for my testimonial game against Derby County

My testimonial programme

CHAPTER TEN
A night I'll always remember

With top-flight players earning so much money these days, many people think that testimonials are a little outdated. But they are still a vital source of income for some loyal, lower-league players who are coming towards the end of their careers. I enjoy playing in testimonials and turned out in matches for Stuart Pearce, where I even scored a goal, Des Walker and Steve Chettle.

I was certainly grateful when I was offered one at Forest, but it was a reward for staying at the club after I turned down the chance to sign for Leeds. I ended up signing a new contract at the City Ground – for less money than Leeds had offered me. I was awarded a testimonial, against Derby County in May 2000, to help make up for the shortfall.

A testimonial year might sound like good fun, but it's bloody hard work, I can tell you. My wife, Gaynor, was pregnant with our son Tommy so she couldn't help me. Fortunately, I had a great committee, led by Ron Parker, who worked tirelessly on my behalf. We had a night at the dogs, golf days and Q&As.

It was great fun, but I was out of the house a lot. To be honest, I was knackered at the end of it and it was a bit of a relief when it was all over. The strain was massive, but it was worth it because we had some fun and I ended up with a good few quid.

One of the first testimonial events was at Jongleurs, a comedy club in Nottingham. David Platt had just joined the club as manager and it was going to be the first chance for the fans to meet him.

It was a complete sell-out but, on the afternoon of the event, Platt telephoned me and said he couldn't make it because he was signing Stern John, or something. It left me in the shit, so I went on stage and offered the fans their money back, but they all stayed. Fortunately, some of the Forest lads, like Steve Chettle, Steve Stone, Ian Woan and Colin Cooper, were there to support me and we ended up having a brilliant night with the fans. I never missed a chance to get together with supporters and used to visit branches once a month to join in with quiz nights and other events.

My first choice for opposition were Celtic, but they wanted so much money to come down that it was a non-starter. Fortunately, Jim Smith offered to bring his Derby County side over. Remarkably, he never asked for a penny, not even expenses, which I thought was a great gesture. I was happy it was Derby in the end, because I used to love the banter with Rams fans. Of course they gave me some stick, but I enjoyed giving it back.

I generally got on well with Derby fans – apart from one night at Sam Fayes when I was playing pool with Brett Williams. A Derby fan spat in my face and when I turned round my back was covered in spit as well.

We were playing for money, best of five and were level going into the last game when a fan came over and picked up the white ball. He said he'd done it for a dare. One of my mates, Stan Mitchell, picked him up and threw him on the barbecue outside. By the way, I won 3-2.

As you can imagine, it was an expensive business staging a testimonial match, even in those days. You have to hire the ground, pay for the floodlights and the police.

The police bill alone was over £10,000, because I had to have extra cover with Derby in town. Fortunately, all the stewards offered their services for nothing, which was brilliant.

I had to go over to Derby to see Jim Smith to discuss the game and this set a few tongues wagging. There was even talk that I was signing for the Rams, which didn't go down too well with some Forest fans. But, c'mon, would I?

It was Larry Lloyd who came up with the fantastic idea of

getting the European Cup-winning team back together on the night. It had never even crossed my mind. The idea was that they would come on for 15 minutes after the main game, which was all some of them could manage to be fair, and play my All Stars side, which included the likes of Paul Merson, Ian Wright, John Barnes and, of course, Vinnie Jones.

They flew from all over the world to be there that night, apart from Trevor Francis who, unfortunately, had other commitments. The turnout was absolutely amazing and I really can't thank them enough.

Obviously, I wanted Brian Clough to come to the game, which he agreed to do. But he took some getting hold of and I eventually had to go round his house.

I took Lilli with me and knocked on his door. He popped his head round the corner and must have known why I was there because, before I could say a word, he shouted: "Shithouse, the answer is Yes, I'll be there. Now piss off and get off my land."

The only problem was that I was not allowed to advertise that the great man would be there until a week before the game. When I finally went on television and radio to announce that the European Cup-winning team would be there, along with Brian Clough, everything went crazy.

I was expecting about 8,000 fans to turn up, and to be honest, I would have been happy with that, considering that I had been on the bench a lot that season as cover for Dave Beasant.

Ten minutes before the kick-off, a police inspector came into the dressing room. He had some good news and some bad news! The bad news was that the kick-off would have to be delayed for at least ten minutes. My heart sank and I immediately thought trouble had kicked off between the rival fans. But the good news was that around 18,000 fans were trying to get into the ground and they were still swarming over Trent Bridge.

Obviously the turnout that night was down to Brian Clough and the old boys. BC came on the pitch carrying the European

Cup, gave me a kiss and a hug and told me not to forget to send him his share.

He had a very good friend called Colin, who I saw from time to time, so I told him I would give Cloughie fifty quid. But I never did. Looking back, I should have posted it to him.

The best thing was that David Platt was sitting in Cloughie's old seat in the directors' box and Ron Parker, who was chairman of the Testimonial Committee, went and told him he would have to move and make way for the gaffer. I bet that went down well with Platty!

But it was a night I will treasure for the rest of my life. It was unbelievable; so emotional because I knew that, pretty soon, I would be leaving the club. It makes the hair stand up on the back of my neck just thinking about it now.

It was a real carnival atmosphere that night and much of it was a blur, but I do remember Paul Merson chipping a cracker past Derby 'keeper Mart Poom from about 25-yards.

The All Stars were Crossley, Laws, Walker, Chettle, Thomas, Merson, Barnes, Clough, Jemson, Waddle, Jones, Fletcher, Woan, Harewood, Rogers, Johnson, Downes, Pembridge.

Derby County: Poom, Oakes, Laursen, Delap, Elliott, Schnoor, Dorigo, Johnson S, Bohinen, Murray, Burley, Kinkladze, Burton, Christie, Jackson, Riggott, Le Geyt, Bolder.

The European Cup winners were: Woods, Shilton, O'Neill, Clark, Gemmill, Bowyer, Woodcock, Birtles, Mills, Gunn, Lloyd, Burns, McGovern, Robertson.

Afterwards we all had a party in the Jubilee Club. It was great end to a truly memorable night and I never wanted it to end.

The only downside was, I knew I had to start looking for a new club, after David Platt kindly withdrew the offer of a new contract.

That last day at the City Ground was one of the worst days of my life. I was having to leave the club that I loved and there was nothing I could do about it. Just coming to the ground to pick up my stuff was emotional for me. Driving down to the ground for the last time ranks among the worst moments of my career.

The one consolation was that I had got a couple of internationals with Wales coming up, including one against Brazil and that took my mind off things a bit.

Forest was a big part of my life and it broke my heart when I drove into the City Ground to pack up my stuff and say my goodbyes to the staff. That included the lady who once sewed my pockets up.

Brian Clough was always telling me off for standing with my hands in my pockets. One day he caught me and dragged me along to the drying room, where the kit was drying on red-hot pipes, and told the lady to sew my pockets up. He always wanted you to look smart, clean shaven and with your hair cut short.

Anyway, I put my boots in a black bin bag and that was it. It was only when I sat in the bath at home that night that it dawned on me. After 13 years at the City Ground it was all over.

I got invited back to the City Ground for a game against Derby, which was great, and I went back there to play for Fulham in the FA Cup. We had just beaten Birmingham and I couldn't believe it when Forest (away) came out in the draw.

I said to the Fulham manager, Chris Coleman, that I had to play in that game and I did. But I must say that it was weird playing for the opposition at the City Ground.

Gareth Taylor missed a sitter in the final minutes and we went on to win in extra time. I certainly had divided loyalties that day and I probably would not have minded that much if Forest had won.

What a night! The European Cup winners turn out for my testimonial game

The European Cup winners made it a night that I will never forget

Going for goal in Stuart Pearce's testimonial match at the City Ground

Yes, that really is me scoring in Steve Chettle's testimonial game

A quick word with Des Walker during his testimonial match

A black day as I leave the City Ground for good

I often think what would have happened if I had signed for Martin O'Neill

CHAPTER ELEVEN
From Cold Blow Lane to a pig farm

One day, while I was with the family at Center Parcs, I got a call saying Martin O'Neill wanted me at Leicester. That would have been a great move for me because he offered me £10,000 a week and it meant I wouldn't have to leave Nottingham. They wanted me and I wanted to go, so we shook hands and the deal was done. But, the following day, Martin was offered the job at Celtic. He couldn't take me with him because Celtic already had three 'keepers. So it was back to square one for me.

I played a waiting game that summer, but I started to panic because there was nothing on the horizon. I had an offer from Scotland and agreed a deal with Hibs manger Alex McLeish.

Believe it or not, I was on my way to the airport to sign when right out of the blue, I got a call from Bryan Robson, who I had met briefly when I was on loan at Manchester United. He wanted me to sign for Middlesbrough. He told me to call Hibs and pretend I'd got a puncture or that the car had broken down on the way to the airport.

I didn't fancy breaking the news to Alex so I took the coward's way out and left it to my agent, Ian Elliott. I was bang out of order. I am sure that if I had told him in person he would have understood my position. But what could I do?

Hibs offered me £4,000 a week, but Middlesbrough were prepared to pay me, at my age, £7,000 a week, plus another £2,000 appearance money. There was no way I could turn that down. Plus, the facilities there were great. They had a state-of-the-art indoor pitch, a gym and, just as important for me, a brilliant goalkeeping coach in Paul Barron.

I didn't really want to live in Middlesbrough because I had heard bad reports about it. As it happens it was a great place and

I really enjoyed going out there. The folks were like me – down to earth and mad! Believe it or not, I lived on a pig farm near Thirsk. A friendly estate agent, who happened to be a 'Boro fan, put me on to it, he said it was a bargain at £295,000. I thought he was mad but it turned out he was spot on.

The smell of the pigs was a bit ripe, I can tell you. But the farm was going downhill fast. There were only about 70 pigs left and they went within six months. There were just a few goats, which the kids loved. I spent about £10,000 on lighting and security for the U-shaped barn conversion and was delighted when I sold it for £525,000 two years later. It turned out to be the best investment I've ever made.

The only problem was that I was going to Middlesbrough as No.2 to Mark Schwarzer. I was confident I could get in the team even though he was a very good 'keeper. At the end of the day, I think I helped make him an even better player, because he had never had anyone pushing him before I arrived. It was the same with Edwin van der Sar when I was at Fulham.

I enjoyed my three seasons at Middlesbrough, even though I nearly got killed in training one day. There was a massive bolt in the wall in the gym with elastic attached to it. It was designed to improve your strength and was so supposed to be so strong that it could stand the pull of two tractors. But when I ran to the first cone the bolt suddenly came away from the wall and hit me in the back.

I was out of action for about a month. The lads were pissing themselves, until they realised that if the bolt had hit me on the back of the head it would have killed me.

The trouble was, I never really got much chance to show what I could do at Middlesbrough and I never even made an appearance in 2002-03, when Mark Schwarzer was ever-present.

When I arrived in 2000-01 Schwarzer and Gary Walsh were the 'keepers and it was nine matches before I got a look in. But things didn't go according to plan. Unfortunately, we lost 3-1 at home to Newcastle in front of a bumper crowd of 31,436 and we also lost to Charlton (0-1), Ipswich (1-2) and Arsenal (0-1) before Schwarzer came back into the side. I remember the defeat at Ipswich, because my poor clearance gifted a goal to Richard Naylor. I was normally good in those situations, but this time I completely missed my kick.

It didn't get much better in the home game with Arsenal, who fielded the likes of Martin Keown, John Lukic, Dennis Bergkamp, Lee Dixon, Patrick Vieira and Tony Adams. It was our fifth straight defeat. Gary Pallister's poor pass after 22 minutes put me in trouble and I brought down Freddie Ljungberg, who was through on goal. I dived at his feet and he went over my arm. A red card from Andy D'Urso and a penalty, which Thierry Henry put away. Thank you very much.

Marlon Beresford came on and made some great saves, but the pressure was now on Bryan Robson after he had spent £18m on new players in just three months. Players like Croatian World Cup striker Alen Boksic came in as chairman Steve Gibson splashed the cash. It turned out that Boksic, who arrived from Lazio for a massive £2,500,000, was one of the highest paid players in the League. But he suffered with injuries, which limited his appearances, and he had to retire in 2003.

Alen was so laid back that he'd stub his cigarette out at the door and arrive about five minutes before training was due to start. One day he left his wage slip lying around and we couldn't resist having a quick look. We couldn't quite believe our eyes. He was on over £65,000 a week, after tax. But he repaid a bit of that with two goals on his debut against Coventry City and was the club's leading scorer that season with twelve goals.

In 2001-02, I made a total of 17 appearances, plus one as sub. We finished 12th in the league, but the lack of firepower was illustrated by the fact that Alen Boksic was leading scorer with eight goals, and two of those were penalties.

I replaced Mark Schwarzer in the seventh match of the

season, the 2-2 draw at Chelsea. We were two down at the break, but earned a point with goals from Stockdale and a last-minute Boksic penalty. Chelsea had the likes of Melchiot, Terry, Desailly, Gallas, Zenden, Lampard and Hasselbaink on show. They had such a good side that Zola and Le Saux were on the bench.

I was at fault with the first goal. I came out to block a pass from Gudjohnson, but Jimmy Floyd beat me to the ball. Seven minutes before the break he did me again.

I felt I did well in the 0-0 draw at Charlton. I just wanted to prove to myself that I could still do it and those couple of games did my confidence the world of good, but Steve McClaren, who had taken over from Robson in July, brought Schwarzer back for the next three games against Sunderland, Spurs and Derby, who were beaten 5-1.

McClaren did a good job for 'Boro. I got on well with him. I rated him, both as a coach and manager and had the utmost respect for him. Now I am a coach myself I understand things a little better.

I finally got a decent run in the side, playing thirteen games in a row, keeping six clean sheets in the process.

I kept successive clean sheets against Villa, Ipswich and Blackburn and was really looking forward to the big game with Liverpool at Anfield. Unfortunately, I lasted only 16 minutes and exited on a stretcher with concussion after blocking Gary McAllister.

I came out low to try and save as Gary slid in. As he went past me he caught me just above the temple with his elbow and left a big hole in my head. It was a pure accident. Just one of those things that can happen in football. I wanted to come back on, but the injury was worse than I thought and it needed eight stitches. In the end, we lost 2-0.

On December 15 we lost 1-0 at home to Manchester United. We were destroyed by Ryan Giggs; we just couldn't get the ball off him. After all, he was one of the best players in the world. The only goal came after 75 minutes. I palmed out a cross from Giggs and Van Nistelrooy did the rest. I was disappointed because I desperately wanted to do well. My contract was up at the end of the season, my family were settled and I didn't want to leave. But I was 32 and I needed to be playing regular first-team football. Plus, I wanted to get my place in the Welsh team for the European Championships qualifiers.

On New Year's Day, I played in the 1-0 home win over Everton. I was injured again, after only 15 minutes, but I recovered to keep out headers from Alan Stubbs and big Duncan Ferguson. The bar also saved me, but we deserved the win courtesy of Gianluca Festa.

It got even better when we beat Manchester United 2-0 at The Riverside in the FA Cup. It was then that tragedy struck Colin Cooper, who had a lovely family. His two-year-old son choked to death hours after the match. I was absolutely devastated for them.

I had played 14 games in a row and was in the form of my life, keeping eight clean sheets as we shot up the League. So I was shocked, to say the least, when Mark Schwarzer was brought back for the 1-0 FA Cup win over Blackburn.

It pissed the crowd off as well. They liked Mark, but they had also taken to me and knew what was happening just wasn't right. After a couple of days the shock turned to anger. I was upset because I felt that I had done more than enough to warrant a place in the team and had been treated unfairly. It was clear to me that I was now regarded as nothing more than a No.2 at the Riverside.

My run in the side ended with the 2-2 draw at home to Leeds. We were 2-0 down at the break, but hit back to salvage a point through Paul Ince and Dean Windass. Unfortunately, I missed the next six games but came back for the 1-1 draw with Spurs and the 1-0 win at Derby who were sunk by a goal from Robbie

Mustoe after just 12 minutes. I have to say, the support from the fans was brilliant. When you have the fans on your side like that, it's difficult to leave a club. It was the same for me at Forest.

So I decided to sign a new two-year deal, despite offers from other clubs at home and abroad. That's when I learned a valuable lesson about agents. Chris Waddle had put me in touch with a new agent called Ian Elliott. As you will have gathered, I'm not a big fan of some agents and I know they often get a bad press, but Ian is a great bloke and we have never had a contract.

Unfortunately, he sold his business and went to work for a bigger company. I was about to sign my new contract at 'Boro when the secretary asked me if I knew this company was taking £55,000 off me.

I said: "No way. It's the first I've heard of it." Needless to say, they didn't get the money and my agent left the company in protest. It just shows how careful you have to be.

One of the other big names at 'Boro during my time there was French World Cup star Christian Karembeu, who arrived from Real Madrid in 2000. He was married to a stunning Slovak model called Adriana Sklenarikova. Neil Maddison had pictures of her in his private locker, which was next to Karembeu's. Neil used to wait for Christian to come in, open the locker door and go "She's fit" just to wind him up. You should have seen the look on his face.

By now, I was getting great coaching from Paul Barron and Stephen Pears and I was starting to reap the benefits. It was something I had never had in my career before. I was 100% pre-pared for anything by kick-off time. I was the fittest I had ever been.

A lady physio in Nottingham sorted my back out with some stretching exercises and I will always be grateful to her for that. She probably saved my career and I owe her a big debt. My all-round game had improved and I was getting extra distance on my kicks. But I needed first-team football, so I jumped at the chance to join Stoke on loan....even though they were bottom of the table and favourites for the drop at the time.

But the record books show that I kept seven clean sheets in eleven games .... and they stayed up. Their manager, Tony Pulis, went on record as saying I was one of the top five signings he ever made.

I liked him. I liked the way he managed. He was dedicated and didn't stand any nonsense from the players. It's a pity there aren't more managers like him around today.

I really loved my time there and I suppose I helped save him from the sack. They had a great fan base, 14,000 or more, even though they were struggling, and they really took to me.

It certainly boosted my confidence and gave me a new lease of life. Tony wanted to sign me, but Middlesbrough called me back after one game, a 1-1 draw at Gillingham, because Mark Schwarzer was injured. But, to my surprise, he suddenly declared himself fit on the Friday morning....so I was back out on loan to Stoke again.

I kept clean sheets in the draws with Ipswich, Sheffield Wednesday and Wolves. On a nice little run now, Stoke won 2-1 at Watford with two from Peter Hoekstra, one from the penalty spot and drew 0-0 with Gillingham.

Warhurst and Cooke scored in the 2-0 home win over Rotherham and, although we lost 3-1 at Millwall, we beat Wimbledon (2-1) and Coventry and Reading 1-0. Ade Akinbyi got the vital goal in the last game of the season in front of a crowd of 20,477. Stoke finished 21st in the league and were safe. What an escape!

I was on fire for a while at Middlesbrough and loving every minute of it when Steve McClaren took over.

Then he let me down a bit and brought Schwarzer back – even though I was playing out of my skin. The day I found out I was dropped, I went home – I must admit, I lost it for a while. Paul Barron could see I was upset and followed me home. We sat for about an hour and talked. I still speak to him on a regular basis. I was playing for the reserves every week, even though a few clubs wanted me on loan. Middlesbrough rated me highly. Unfortunately, not highly enough.

I had a year left on my contract at Middlesbrough when Steve Bruce, who was manager at Birmingham at the time, came in for me. The problem was Middlesbrough wanted £500,000 for me. Birmingham wanted to pay it over three years, but 'Boro were asking for it all upfront. I then heard that the price had gone up to £750,000 and the deal was off.

It bugged me that they had denied me the chance to play for Birmingham. After all, Middlesbrough never paid a penny for me and here they were asking for a small fortune.

They signed Carlo Nash to replace me for nothing, so why ask a big fee for me? I had to get away. Fortunately, my old Wales team-mate, Chris Coleman, came to the rescue....

Curtis Fleming protests, but it's a red card for me

I was never happy being a second-choice 'keeper

All in a day's work. loved visiting the local schools

Playing for Fulham against my old club, Forest

CHAPTER TWELVE
The bright lights of London

Chris Coleman called me and asked if I was going to Birmingham, but I told him I thought it had fallen through. He said that Maik Taylor would probably be going to St Andrews and he wanted me to replace him. In the end Chris paid £500,000 to take me to Fulham as No.2 to Edwin van der Sar, but assured me there was no way Edwin would be at the club much longer – he would soon be off to a bigger club, like Manchester United.

Barnsley, the club I always wanted to play for, and Leeds (again) were interested. But I could not believe the deal Chris put on the table. Birmingham had offered £7,000 and £2,000 appearance money. But Chris was prepared to give me £10,000 and £2,000 appearance money, plus a £100,000 signing-on fee – just for sitting on the bench! It sounds a lot of money, but not that unusual for moving to a club in London.

London, I couldn't wait. I was staying in a lovely hotel near Wimbledon Common. I thought my wife and kids would love it there. Chris Coleman is a great guy. He looked after me and I have a lot of time for him. Because of my injury problems I had to have a two-day medical and an MRI scan on my dodgy back, but it wasn't a problem.

My first game for the reserves was against Crystal Palace and 'Pudsey', the kit man, went to my son, Tommy, and told him to run onto the pitch and shout to his dad. We had a corner when Tommy, who was four at the time, started to wander onto the pitch shouting "Dad, Dad." I had to dash from my goal and carry him back off.

I made only one appearance in 2003-04 in the 2-1 home defeat by Liverpool. I was used sparingly the following season with just five appearances, plus one as sub, as we finished 13th in the league. We beat Spurs 2-0 at home with goals from Andy Cole and Luis Boa Morte, but lost three in a row to Chelsea (1-4), Everton (1-0) and Blackburn (0-2). I played in all the cup games while Edwin was rested and then I got in the team for the game against Birmingham. We won 1-0 with a goal from Mark Pembridge and I was named Man of the Match. Chris Coleman said: "Make it hard for me to leave you out". So I did. We beat Newcastle 4-1, after they had 29 shots on target, and I was awarded ten out of ten in The Sun newspaper, which was un-heard of for a goalkeeper in those days. I was quite proud of that.

Edwin was a great 'keeper, but he wasn't a great talker or organiser back then. And I think I helped him with that. Looking back, I think I helped improve his game. We became quite close in the end. I had a time-share in Portugal and when he was playing for Holland in the European championships we met up for a meal and a chat at the gorgeous Pine Cliff resort where the Dutch team were staying.

The next morning I went to fetch my paper when who should be coming the other way....only my old mate Pierre van Hooij-donk. I made a swift left turn. There was no way I wanted to talk to him. I felt bad for blanking him – for about two seconds. But it was probably for the best because I still hadn't forgiven him.

I was happy with my form at Fulham, but I was having problems with my marriage. Gaynor wasn't happy and things started to go from bad to worse. We ended up sleeping in seperate beds.

At the end of the season I took my mum, dad and the kids to a villa in Spain with Steve Stone, Lee Clarke, Steve Watson and their families. It was one of the best holidays I have ever had and they really helped me through my marriage problems. I began to get over the break up and finally started to relax a little. Plus, Edwin was off to Manchester United, just as Chris said he would.

Things started to look up even more when I got a call from

Chris saying I was going to be the No.1 'keeper. I had a new contract worth £12,000 a week, plus £3,000 appearance money, and £750 a point win bonus. Tony Warner started the season in goal but, after seven games, I came in for the home game with Manchester United. Unfortunately, we lost 3-2 despite goals from Collins John and Claus Jensen. We drew 1-1 at Charlton and beat Liverpool 2-0 at home through John and Boa Morte before the injury jinx struck again and I was out for three games. I was doing well until I was injured again in the 3-2 defeat at Chelsea. I played in the next game, a 3-3 draw at home to Villa, but tore my hamstring for the fourth time by trying to rush back too quickly. There was a 10cm tear, it was serious, and I missed the next eleven games.

Chris knew he had to go out and sign a new 'keeper, after all, this could have been the end of my career. I was disappointed, but I knew where he was coming from. I also had to have a cartilage operation on my knee in 2004. Fortunately, Mr. Al Fayed has his own surgeon, Fares Haddad, who did a great job and I've never had a problem since.

On the plus side, that's when I first got interested in being a manager. Chris let me sit in his office and see how the club worked, how to deal with players and agents and things like that. I thought: 'This is the way forward for me. I want to be a coach/manager one day. This is something I can do when I retire.'

Andy Cole was at Fulham while I was there. Some people said he could be a bit funny, but I got on OK with him. I think I made him laugh. He had so much talent and ability and his finishing was deadly. He was a pleasure to watch.

Andy was a great player, but one of the best strikers I have played with was Louis Saha. He could have been world class had he not suffered badly from injuries. He has everything, pace, power and two great feet. He was also good in the air and a great finisher in the right formation.

In my first season at Fulham, we finished ninth in the League and a lot of that was down to the brilliance of Louis Saha. When Manchester United came in with a £15m bid for him, he was on his way. There was no way Fulham could turn that kind of money down.

I again found myself as the second-choice 'keeper, this time to the flying Fin Antti Niemi, who also had a good record for saving penalties at the time. He went on to become goalkeeping coach to the Finland team when he retired through injury.

I had a cracker in my comeback game, the 1-0 home win over Chelsea. I made three or four outstanding saves from Damian Duff in the first half before we took the lead with a fluke from Louis Boa Morte.

Then Didier Drogba got away with a crafty hand-ball as he went past me and rolled the ball into the empty net. Luckily we protested and the 'goal' was disallowed. With just seconds to go Chelsea were awarded a corner and John Terry got in a free header which I managed to turn over the bar.

It was the first time Fulham had beaten their local rivals, who boasted a team worth over £300 million, in years.

I also kept a clean sheet in the draw with Villa. But we lost 3-1 at home to Portsmouth and I suddenly found myself down the pecking order again behind Niemi and a Czech 'keeper called Jan Lastuvka. I was depressed after my marriage to Gaynor broke up, living on my own in a flat getting and pissed two or three nights a week.

I piled into training at Fulham as I tried to get my sanity back. I was training twice a day and also going swimming. The fitness coach was an Australian called Steve Nance and he helped me a lot. He designed an arm bike and a boxing routine and I got down to 11% body fat. I had never felt fitter. I was training hard with Mark Pembridge, who was also injured at the time.

Having said that, Tuesday nights out at Fulham were some-thing special. We went to a place called Secrets, which was a lap-dancing bar. We used to go there for the first drinks at nine o'clock before we went into London and partied until four or five in the morning at the Funky Budha night club.

We had some great meals at Fulham with Mr Al Fayed being there, because they were prepared by a chef from Harrods. I didn't put on any weight because I was eating so healthily and not calling in at McDonald's on the way home!

Mr Al Fayed, who rescued Fulham from the scrap heap in 1997, used to land his helicopter on the training pitch and then emerge surrounded by bodyguards. He once brought Michael Jackson into the dressing room at QPR and said: "Cover your willies lads, Michael Jackson is here." I couldn't believe it was happening. But Michael was very shy and when he came in he never said a word.

One good thing about Mr Al Fayed was that at Christmas he treated us all to a hamper from Harrods, it must have been worth £1,000. One year we beat Manchester United, Arsenal and Chelsea before Christmas and, as a reward, he sent us FOUR hampers. That took care of the Christmas shopping for me; I never had to buy a present, which was handy.

When I was at Fulham I met a girl in a club and we had a bit of a fling. It turned out to be the daughter of my old Forest team-mate Brian Laws. What are the chances of that? When I found out who she was I telephoned Brian straight away.

Unfortunately, it was about two in the morning and I got him out of bed! As fate would have it, he took me on loan from Fulham, which could have been a bit awkward.

I joined Sheffield Wednesday on loan two days into Brian's reign. It was handy for me because I could stay with my mum and dad.

The rest of the time I was in a hotel which was only ten minutes from the training ground. They were struggling a bit, but I soon became a talisman with the fans. I made my debut at Ipswich Town in front of over 21,000 fans and we won 2-0.

We lost the next game, 3-1 at Coventry, but I had a great game, and then drew 0-0 at home with Cardiff. I made a point-blank save with a couple of minutes to go. We then chalked up three wins in a row, but my hamstrings were playing me up. I was only 65% fit and my form dipped as a result.

My champagne moment came when we were trailing 3-2 in the home game with Southampton. I went up for a last-minute corner and even surprised myself when I headed it in. I'd been close to a goal with Fulham before, when I went up for a corner against Wigan. I hit a volley from the edge of the box, but their Aussie goalkeeper, John Fillan, pulled off a great save.

This time, I was looking at the bench for a sign, should I go or should I stay? So I thought, bugger it and off I trotted. It was the thought of getting back that worried me. And, because of my hamstring niggle, it crossed my mind that if I went up I might not be able to get back. In the end, I didn't really have time to jump, I just timed my run rose like a salmon and the ball landed on my head. That's the advantage of having a big head, I suppose.

I'd gone 480 games without a goal, so I suppose I was long overdue one – although I did blast in a penalty in the 3-3 draw with Mansfield in a testimonial for their long-serving secretary Joe Eaton and I scored after coming on as a striker in Steve Chettle's testimonial match.

I played 45 minutes up front in Stuart Pearce's testimonial and scored as the Forest X1 won 6-5. I was determined to score and every time the ball came near me I just hammered it towards the goal. Fortunately, I got one in the end. But this one for Wednesday was a proper goal. It was a great feeling when the ball hit the back of the net, I can tell you. Mind you, the hamstring was screaming at me by the time I got back to the other end. It was a good job I did score, because I was at fault with their second goal when I was beaten in the air by Kenwyn Jones. I was obviously delighted, but I was pleased for the fans as much as anything. I built up a great understanding with them in my short time there. I loved every minute of it to be honest.

That FA Cup Final save was obviously very special, but that goal against Southampton was right up there with the magic moments.

The sheer passion of the Sheffield Wednesday supporters is amazing. I've played at some great clubs over the years, but the Wednesday fans were really amazing, especially away from home. One of them, Sam Salim, who was an Owls fanatic, used to chaffeur me around.

Next up was a trip to Stoke and I got a great reception from the fans, even though we won 2-1. By contrast, I got some grief at my hometown club, Barnsley, where we won 3-0 with goals from Andrews, Brunt and MacLean.

But we then went seven games without a win. The writing was on the wall for me and my last game was the 3-2 defeat at Luton. Sadly, two of the goals were down to me and I tried to make amends by going up for a corner, but I flicked the ball just wide this time. On the Thursday morning we were in the gym and Brian called me over for a word and said he wasn't renewing my contract. Brian said he was bringing Iain Turner in, so I found myself on the way back to London. He said it was the hardest decision he ever had to make.

When I went to Wednesday, the deal was that if I played 20 games I would get a contract for another year. I'd even started looking at houses in the area. But they left me out when I'd made 17 League appearances.

Coventry wanted me on loan, but Wednesday, who had been paying half my wages, would not release my registration for some reason. I was training Monday to Friday, but not playing for anyone come Saturday. The upshot was that I was going home to Barnsley and going on the piss.

I thought my playing days were over and my head had gone again. I was staying with my mum and dad and they were going mad at me. I couldn't go on like that. I was heading for trouble again. I was out of contract at the end of the 2006-07 season and Fulham released me. I had an offer from Darlington, but I was 37 going on 38 with back and hamstring problems, only training twice a week.

When Chris Coleman got the sack, Irish international Lawrie Sanchez, who had been managing Northern Ireland very successfully, came in for a brief spell. I was looking for a hint about the future from him, but he never said anything. In his first team talk he said: "I might get the team wrong first time, but I will not get it wrong the second time." But, at the end of the day, I thought he was just a stop-gap. I was playing in the reserves, so I didn't have much time to get to know him. Training wasn't great, especially as we had been taken by Steve Kean, one of the best coaches I have worked with.

In the end, Lawrie won one game on the final day of the season, thanks to a last-minute penalty against Newcastle, and we stayed up. He quit Northern Ireland, after taking them from 124th in the world to 27th, to take the Fulham job, but won only four of his 24 games in charge and was soon on his way.

I had the chance to go to America when I left Fulham. An agent sounded me out, but it never went any further than that. I still felt I had a lot to offer. I had suffered a lot of injuries and didn't want to risk going over there and getting injured so far away from home. May be one day I'll get to coach over there. I also had the offer of a coaching job at QPR with John Gregory. I met him in an hotel and my first impressions of the man were good. We got on great and I think it could have worked. Lee Camp was goalkeeper at QPR at the time and I would have liked to have worked with him.

John offered me £40,000 which was tempting because I was back in London and closer to my kids. But the trouble was I wasn't quite ready. The timing was all wrong. Basically, I felt I could still play.

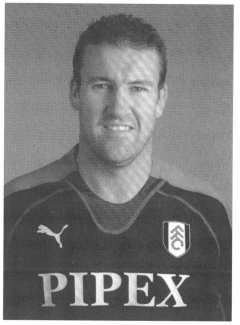

I had to pay for this shirt after ripping the neck

Happy days during my time at Fulham

The kids get into the party mood at a family day at Fulham

Golden goal: A champagne moment as I go up for a corner

He leaps, he soars, he scores and Gareth Bale can only look on

What a wonderful feeling......

Suddenly I'm a hero again

Getting a little heavier as the years tick by

CHAPTER THIRTEEN
A storm in a tea cup

It was then that yet another face from the past arrived on the scene. John Sheridan had only been at Nottingham Forest for three months, after turning down Chelsea to go to the City Ground, before Brian Clough dumped him.

It was unbelievable. He'd just had a great game in the Little-woods Cup, but I think he upset the gaffer one day when he tried to chip the 'keeper and he was soon on his way.

John and me hit it off straight away and when the offer to join him at League One Oldham came along, I jumped at the chance.

It was an ideal move for me as I was determined to get all my coaching badges so I could move into management one day. We got on well and our families went on holiday together.

He offered me £1,500 a week, plus appearances money, to join him as player-coach. But it wasn't about the money this time. To be honest, I was lonely living alone in my flat and wanted to get closer to home – even though I knew I'd miss my children.

I had two great years at Boundary Park and only missed a handful of games in my first season. I played 59 League games in all. Don't ask me how I kept fit. At Middlesbrough we had three full-time masseurs, three full-time physios, three fitness gurus, nutritionists, two doctors, plus specialists for ankles, backs and knees. You name a part of the body and we had a spe-cialist for it. At Oldham we had a bucket of cold water, a sponge and a tin of plasters! The bottom line was, you couldn't afford to get injured.

In my first season at Boundary Park we finished 8th in the table. We won the opening game, at home to Swansea, 2-1 with a penalty from Michael Ricketts and a last-minute goal from

Craig Davies. But we lost the next four, three of them 1-0, so we were soon up against it. But we bounced back to beat Walsall 3-0 and Crewe 3-2, this time with a last-gasp goal from Neil Kilkenny.

I played in the 1-1 draw at Cheltenham, but then sat out the next five games, missing the trip to my old club, Forest, into the bargain because of a thigh strain.

I came back for the 1-1 draw at home to Port Vale and we went on a nice little run of seven games unbeaten until we lost 2-0 at home to Walsall.

We only lost seven more games after that, putting four goals past Huddersfield and Crewe. I missed three games in March, but ended up making 38 appearances which gave me a great deal of satisfaction.

One of the highlights was the 1-0 win in the FA Cup at Everton in front of 5,000 travelling fans in January 2008. David Moyes sent out a weakened side and we did him with a 25-yard goal from Gary McDonald. But we went out at home in the 4th round, 1-0 at home to Huddersfield.

To be honest, I thought days like this had gone for me, with my career winding down as it was. To come to a Premier League club and win was something special. I think it got us a massive £75 win bonus.

It was a different world now. I had been used to going into training and being handed clean kit. We had to wash our own kit and look after our own boots, which, looking back, wasn't such a bad thing. We paid £8 a month for a meal twice a week after training, a jacket potato and a bit of chilli.

There is an old saying that a fool and his money are soon parted. One day a bloke in a video van pulled up at the ground and asked directions to a nearby industrial estate. He said he was delivering to Argos.

He thanked us and asked if we would be interested in buying a cam-corder cheap. They cost £350 but he would let us have them for £150. I said that I was definitely interested at the price and the gaffer said he'd have one as well. I don't normally carry large sums of money on me, after being robbed of £600 when I was at Forest. No-one was ever caught (although I did have my suspicions). Fortunately, the chairman, Maurice Rowarth, went out of his way to make sure that I got reimbursed. But for some reason, that day I did have some with me. I paid for three of them and thought I'd got a right good bargain until one of the lads took a closer look at them and discovered they were duds. I'd just forked out £450 on a pile of junk.

We started the 2008-09 season well beating Millwall 4-3 with two goals from Andy Liddell, one from the penalty spot, Leeds 2-0 away and Cheltenham 4-0 at home. After eight games without defeat we went to Stockport and lost 3-1, but hit back to beat Hereford 4-0 through Lee Hughes, Jones, Whitaker and another penalty from Liddell.

Successive 2-0 defeats at Bristol Rovers and Swindon set us back a bit, but Lee Hughes was starting to hit the target and we beat Northampton (1-0), Southend (2-1) and Walsall (3-2). On December 6, we drew 1-1 at home to Brighton and, sadly, that turned out to be my last game for the club.

Money was tight at Oldham and I had the chance to join Glenn Roeder and Lee Clark as goalkeeping coach at Norwich. Oldham would have pocketed £25,000 compensation and got me off their wage bill. Plus, John could have used the extra cash to bring a new player in, so it was a cracking deal for them. I think the owners wanted me to go, but John left the final decision to me.

I was tempted I must say but, in the end, I decided to stay. I had just moved into a new house and didn't want to move even further away from my kids again.

John played on until he was 41 and did a great job for Oldham. It was a big shock when he got the sack because we had been top of the league and were still fourth or fifth at the time.

He doesn't talk about it, but obviously something must have gone on with him and the chairman. Three players – incidentally with the same agent – were signed pre-season that John wasn't keen on.

The situation wasn't helped by the now infamous team-bonding session at Manchester dogs. It didn't help when Lee Hughes and Sean Gregan turned up pissed. The players were mixing with the fans and a great time was being had by all. Lee Hughes was hugging people, as he does, but unfortunately dropped the daughter of one of the directors and she banged her head. Gregen then got a bit out of order and I ushered the pair of them out of the private box we were in.

It was nothing really, just high spirits. There was no head butting the manager, no fighting, no malice involved at all. But a few days later it was splashed all over the papers. They made out it had all kicked off between Sean Gregan and £1m-rated winger Chris Taylor and that Hughesy had the gaffer in a headlock. But I was there. Believe me, it didn't happen. It was simply blown out of all proportion.

It didn't help that we lost 1-0 to Colchester and 6-2 at MK Dons with a weakened team. But maybe this was just the excuse the club were looking for to get rid of John. I told the club that I would stay until the end of the season or they could pay me up. It was their choice. But I was surprised when they asked me to put in my CV for the manager's job.

I was a 5-2 chance with the bookies along with ex-Latics striker Frankie Bunn and former Stockport boss Jim Gannon. I didn't do anything behind John's back and he was with me every step of the way. He told me to go for it because it was a great opportunity at that stage of my career. But, looking back, I was wrong. I should have walked away with him the same day.

At the end of the day it was Oldham that suffered. They only won one more game, but still finished tenth. If John had stayed they would have got promoted. I'm convinced of that....

My son Tommy was the mascot. I hoped he'd bring us luck

The successful Chesterfield FC team from 2010-11

Barnet was a bit tense as you can see, but the Barnsley game in pre-season was a bit of a yawn to be fair

CHAPTER FOURTEEN
A new ground and a new start

In 2009 I jumped at the chance to join John Sheridan and Tommy Wright at Chesterfield. I would have gone almost anywhere with them, but this had the advantage of being local. John was up against Colin Calderwood for the job, but he got the nod. He stopped off at my dad's house and asked if I wanted to go with him. He offered me £30,000 and £10,000 as a player.

It was ideal for me, just being 35 miles down the motorway and now I could also get my foot in the door as a coach with the reserves. I knew I could bring young Tommy Lee on and he's done so well that he made the PFA Team of the Year. I think I've helped to turn him into the best 'keeper in the league.

I played four games and even saved a penalty in pre-season against Matlock. But my back was knackered, my knees were knackered, in fact everything is knackered. At 40, I think I was one of the oldest players ever to turn out for the club, but I was really struggling with my back again. We kicked off at Torquay, losing 2-0, but pipped Cheltenham 1-0 with a 42nd-minute goal from former Forest striker Jack Lester. But we lost the next two, 2-1 at Lincoln and 1-0 at home to Shrewsbury and that was me done. I think my body was telling me that enough was enough. Some of the crowd had been giving me stick and I'd too good a career for that to be happening.

But, I wasn't that bothered because I loved working behind the scenes with John. He is a strong, no-nonsense manager; he doesn't back down or suck up to anyone. A bit like Brian Clough, it's his way or no way. I can't believe Sheffield Wednesday never came in for him when they were looking for a new manager. His passion is unbelievable and he is desperate to do well. I love the way he manages the club and I do see a lot of

Brian Clough in him. He makes training enjoyable with a lot of two-touch and small-sided games.

The boss gives me a fair share of bollockings, but I'm learning from him all the time. It's my job to act as a buffer between the manager and the players, to give lads a lift when things are a bit flat in the dressing room.

I'm happy at Chesterfield, who now have a magnificent new stadium and a superb pitch. I've been for interviews for the manager's jobs at Oldham and Bradford, but I never applied for them, they approached me. The Chesterfield chairman, Barry Hubbard, said he didn't want to lose me, but would not stand in my way. So I went for the interview at Bradford, along with Peter Taylor. I didn't get the job, but it was a good experience.

Last season at Chesterfield we decided to try and bring in players who had performed at a higher level and could still do a job for us. They were all free transfers, they never cost a penny, and it paid off. In fact, I think John has only spent £50,000 since he's been a manager and that was for Craig Davies.

The fans took time to see what John was trying to do but we got promotion at a canter and it's all good at the moment. It's always good to get a promotion on your CV as a coach.

The club is moving forward nicely. All we need now are our own training facilities, which are now in the process of being finished. At the moment we don't have a training base where we can develop young players and attract new faces to the club.

Not that we will have too many problems doing that after the season we have just had. There were something like 800 players out of contract at the end of the season and many will be looking for a new club.

One thing I helped introduce at Chesterfield was the use of sports psychologist Watt Nicoll, who has an uncanny knack of turning weaknesses into strengths. He certainly helped me through my divorce when I felt suicidal and helped give me confidence in myself. He famously gave an inspirational talk to

Kevin Keegan's England team before they went out and beat Poland 3-1. Alan Shearer apparently laughed all the way through it, but I have no hesitation in recommending Watt to other clubs. A former speedway rider and a well-known musician, he is 75 now and has had an amazing life. I owe him a lot.

The 2010-11 season was something special for everyone associated with Chesterfield Football Club. We were the best team in Division Two by a mile. And we won the league by passing the ball. We have shown that you don't have to pump it long to get out of this division. We don't practise set pieces much and play at a high tempo.

After the disappointment of the previous season that saw us drop out of the play-off zone with a few games to go, the summer recruitment drive plus a few terrific signings in mid-season, saw the side score freely and win in style. From mid-October we were top of the league, one odd defeat apart, and we ended the season as truly warranted champions.

The move to a magnificent new stadium saw everyone's expectations exceeded. The Board loved it, so did the management and players and the fans immediately began to feel that the season could be a special one.

As it happened, in winning the title by five points from a top-notch Bury side, the team scored more goals that in any season for more than 50 years, the crowds were the biggest for 30 years and people have been telling me they've never seen a Chesterfield side play like this.

And if you look at some of the other teams, Bury, Wycombe to a certain extent, though they are a little bit more direct, Torquay, Gillingham, Crewe, Accrington Stanley, they all like to try and play football. There's a myth that in this division you have to have a big striker, go long and play in the final third.

Let me tell you, things are changing. The pitch at the B2net has also been massive. Saltergate wasn't bad at all, there were many that were a lot worse, but the surface at our new home looked every bit as good when we did our lap of honour after beating Gillingham in the final match to clinch the trophy and the medals as it did when a Derby County side came to open the ground on a sunny Saturday in July. Groundsman Anthony Haywood was a deserved winner of the Groundsman of the Year Award.

It didn't take long for me to start thinking this could be the year to really kick off things at the club. I thought we looked much improved when we played our pre-season games. You could see we'd got better players in during training sessions, pre-season games and when the season first started.

Our recruitment strategy had been simple. We wanted to bring in players that had played at a higher level that we thought could drop into League Two with no problem. All of them were free transfers or loans, not a penny was spent on transfer fees. We went for the mid-aged, experienced player. That was the philosophy behind it, plus we also wanted players with a winning mentality and a high work ethic. In came Craig Davies and Danny Whitaker, who both made it in to the PFA Team of the Year, along with 'keeper Tommy Lee who'd been Player of the Year in my first season with the club. Tommy was to be challenged by a new face, Shane Redmond, who came in from my previous club, Forest, as I faced up to formally hanging up my gloves, but he saw him off.

Dwayne Mattis and Simon Ford fitted our profile and both went on to have great seasons. Dean Morgan came in after a game or two, he always seems to have so much time on the ball, but was a bit unlucky with a couple of injuries.

Ian Morris returned on loan from Scunthorpe after a spell with us the previous season, while Scott Griffiths was borrowed from Peterborough. Again they met our player specification.

A third loan player came in that didn't meet our requirement. Teenage right-back Jack Hunt, from Huddersfield, had never played in a league game. I know Huddersfield manager Lee

Clark really well and he wouldn't recommend anybody that wasn't any good.

John Sheridan had already seen him play, but his recruitment was like a toss of a coin because of his age and lack of experience. He came in on trial initially and showed in training that he had a little bit about him, a little cockiness and the manager likes that in a player.

Confidence in their own ability is a good thing, particularly in a youngster. We didn't expect Jack to play as many games as he did. He came in as an 'if we need him' type of player, but he grasped his chance. I remember him being gutted when he picked up his fifth booking at Wycombe, meaning he'd miss the Shrewsbury game – a big game at the time – and he was ringing me asking if he'd get back in, just the sort of attitude you want and the type of mentality we've had at the club this season.

When he went back to Huddersfield in January, he was ready made and went straight into their first team, helping them make the play-offs after playing a stormer in a game against Arsenal.

John was criticised the previous season for saying he didn't know what his best side was, but that was just him being typically honest.

We sat in the office time and time again undecided on what was the best side. Obviously John had the final say, but as the recruitment drive came together, all of the pieces of the jigsaw started to paint a picture. And the picture was looking good.

With our motivational coach, the attitude in the dressing room and some good experienced winners to team up with the Jack Lesters, Mark Allotts and Ian Breckins of this world, I felt we'd be right up there.

Our first competitive match of the season was a 2-1 win over a Barnet side that had been completely rebuilt. They didn't know at that stage if they'd be a good team or a poor team, but they worked hard and caused us plenty of problems, particularly after Davies was sent off, but we did enough to win. A disappointing defeat against Gordon Strachan's Middlesbrough (we gave them too much respect in the first half but had a real go at them in the second) was followed by a tough point at Port Vale, where we were second best for an hour. But, like good sides do, we nicked a point.

The supporters got a taste of what was to come with a comprehensive 4-0 win over Hereford United before Davies returned from his suspension to get the first of his 25 goals in a draw at Macclesfield. He has gone to Barnsley and will be hard to replace.

Our brief time in the Johnstone's Paint Trophy though, beating Walsall and then dominating Sheffield Wednesday before losing on penalties, when all 22 players had a kick, showed that next season we've got a chance. Both games were away and I didn't see anything to worry us when we play at that level 46 times in the new season.

We had fewer, but better, players last season and we rotated them quite a bit. Sometimes it paid off, sometimes it didn't. Ironically our only unchanged team was named when we went to Rotherham United and lost 1-0!

But the rotation worked more times than it didn't, though. It was a sort of mini-Premier League system. We've had 20 or so players who the manager knew could all play their part in the team, and they all did. Mattis, Deane Smalley, Morgan, Drew Talbot, Gregor Robertson all proved they could play in a variety of positions and John's treatment of Jack Lester, playing him in all the home games but sparingly away from home, has helped extend his career and he's scored some vital, and stunning, goals at the B2net.

We were putting in a lot of work during the week in training. Let's say we play Wycombe away on a Saturday and we play Stevenage away two weeks later, Stevenage will have watched us and report to their manager, so we tried to use different personnel, different styles of playing, all part of the 'let them worry about us' mentality rather than us worrying about our opponents.

The only time we struggled was when teams put just one up against us and we often struggled to break them down. But when teams want to win, we love it.

Next season that may help. Some of the bigger teams will be coming to 'little Chesterfield' but we'll go at them, attack them and have more than they think in our locker. We'll play the way we want to play and we'll surprise a few.

The season really took off when we played Crewe at home. Dario Gradi is a master at getting players to play the way it should be and after just a few minutes they were 3-0 up and at half-time they led 4-1.

We said at half-time that if there was one team that would give you the chance of coming back, it was Crewe. They can be bullied because they stay honest and continue to play football properly. But that game confirmed the spirit we had and that we can bounce back as young Craig Clay hammered in a last-gasp equaliser to earn a 5-5 draw. A great game, a coach's nightmare, but it was the game that got the crowd believing that anything was possible, and having supporters who believe in you gives a massive boost to everyone.

We were to show that bouncebackability on more than one occasion as the season unfolded. We went top after a 2-1 win at in-form Wycombe in mid-October when Davies scored twice and, barring losing at home to Oxford United after we'd taken the lead, the team was to stay there until May, the only time it truly matters.

I'd like to look back and see how many teams have been top from the middle of October through to the end of a season, sustaining that top spot because you're there to be shot at. The winter weather made that part of the season very bitty with proper training becoming almost impossible at times, but everyone suffered and as the games started to come thick and fast, our squad strength and rotation began to give us a significant advantage. After winning 1-0 at Bradford in February, by which time Deane Smalley and Dean Holden had become vital parts of the squad, we were nine points ahead of second-placed Wycombe and 12 points in front of fourth spot. Things were looking good.

However, it was really difficult for us watching the football shows on television because all of the pundits, for months, were saying we were up. It made Monday mornings a nightmare because we know all of the players would have seen it. We'd have rather everyone say Chesterfield were going well…. that would have made our jobs easier. It's so easy for players to take on board what the pundits say, and when they're saying 'they're up' from about January, it's hard to get everyone focused.

We all know football has a habit of kicking you in the balls when you think the job is done. That's why we've had the motivational coach in and he's been tremendous in his four visits. Those sessions were precious. He left us, as staff, with little things to say to the players.

It says in the dressing room 'Want, Need, Expect.' If you want something, just wanting isn't enough, you've got to need it. The Manchester Uniteds and the Chelseas expect to win every game, so why shouldn't we, and we now expect to win. Believe me, a few words can make a huge difference to a player.

With things going great, we hosted a Morecambe side that, at that time, had forgotten how to win. We lost 2-0. We were booed off at half time by a few of our own supporters, which amazed me, as we were top of the league at the time. But you always get the odd fickle fan everywhere I suppose.

Without doubt, that was the most disappointing part of a great season. It caught us by surprise and, in a way, though it might sound stupid, I'm glad it happened. The defeat and the performance got into the players' psyche and we immediately bounced back to give a great performance against Wycombe, who were the team immediately behind us at the time. We could have easily taken that Morecambe performance into the Wycombe game and lost and then we'd have been on a downward spiral.

As the season went on, the crowd got behind us more and more, although there are always some individuals that dish out generally unfair stick. But the 4-1 win over Wycombe provided the perfect answer.

Wycombe manager Gary Waddock came in afterwards for a beer and simply said that we were the best team they'd played, the same as Paul Buckle at Torquay said, the same as 90% of the opposing managers said after a game. Everyone thought we were up, so keeping level heads was our biggest concern, but we did it pretty well.

Another 2-0 defeat, at Crewe this time (though we were far from disappointed with the performance) was followed by another bounce back, a 5-0 win against promotion rivals Rotherham United that became Ronnie Moore's last game in charge of them. That was the best performance I've seen as a coach in two years at Oldham and two years at Chesterfield and the best performance I've seen from any team in a long time.

But a few days later we were brought back down to earth again, throwing away a two-goal lead at Barnet with their second goal, deep into injury time, coming from a rare misjudgment by Tommy Lee.

I worried after that. l wondered if we were mentally strong enough to sustain it through to the end of the season. It was always a little bit like that, but when you look back now, there were times if we'd have just simply shut up shop, we'd have earned promotion and the title earlier, but it just wouldn't have been us.

We can be a bit gung-ho, we can be a bit cocky, but we genuinely believed throughout the season that we could beat anybody. We perhaps were too gung-ho against Bury in the game that could have clinched the Championship, but we sniffed it there and then and maybe looking back, we should have just settled for a 2-2 draw. But we're just not like that. We want to entertain. Eventually we clinched promotion, without even playing! We knew we were going up after beating Macclesfield in a tense match at home. We came from behind to win with Davies scoring another of his typical belters to level and Whitaker grabbing the winner that had me punching the air knowing promotion by then was a mere formality.

On Good Friday, the day before we were at Oxford, Wycombe went to Torquay and they had to win to prevent us from clinching promotion. I was watching television, keeping up to date with the scores, and when the final result from Plainmoor came on, it was 0-0, we were up.

It was all somewhat subdued. I didn't celebrate because at that stage I knew we'd go up and all of our eyes were on the big prize of the Championship. And that feeling went throughout the camp and was illustrated after our own goalless draw at Oxford.

It was a red-hot day and the fans were brilliant, singing non-stop throughout the game and there was a mini-celebration on the pitch for a few minutes afterwards, when the players were given the 'We're Going Up' flags.

But, in the dressing room afterwards, where the champagne was on ice and ready for popping, the players just sat down quietly, listened to the manager's view on the game and then got changed. No joy, no jumping up and down, no singing. It was really subdued. We didn't want to celebrate then, and credit to the players for that. There were TV cameras in the dressing rooms with Clem from the Football League Show and they had nothing to show for it, no joyous scenes and I bet they were gutted, but we wanted the title.

We'd not won the game, we'd not won a medal, we didn't want to celebrate then, even though we were up. We wanted the top prize. If we'd been second or third all season, bobbing in and out of the top three, it would have been different.

But we'd been top since October, we wanted and needed to

finish top, the job wasn't done until then. Being the best is what we want, how we think, we don't want anything else. We need it.

We were gutted after missing out against Bury in front of a full house at the B2net, but the game, the second half in particular, was a belter, a real credit to both sides. Bury then showed how football is, losing at home to Wycombe after we'd drawn at Torquay, meaning it would all come down to the final day and another packed home crowd.

I always knew it would be tough for Bury at Stevenage, they needed to win but only drew, while we just needed a point against a Gillingham side that needed a result to get into the play-offs. A tense first half was followed by a thrilling final 45 of the season and we deservedly won 3-1, setting up several days of celebrations, though with my partner Emma due to give birth at any moment, I was somewhat more sober than many!

Everyone deserved their success, everyone had worked so hard and the togetherness in the dressing room is as good as it gets.

For me, being a 'keeper, I've been delighted with the progress of Tommy Lee. I'm chuffed to bits how he's come on. And I am going to blow my own trumpet and say that I think I have been a big part of him winning player of the year for two years running and he also reached the PFA team of the year, voted for by the whole of the league's players.

At the end of the previous season, my first season working with him, I sat down and had a chat with him, telling him he needed to improve. As a coach, I can go out there and put training sessions on all day long, I can put Premier League goalkeeper sessions on, no problem, indeed I do that, but 95% of goalkeeping is psychological. How do you recover from a mistake, how do you sustain your form when you're playing well, how do you make yourself better?

I get him to think how could you do this better, do that better and I add my own thoughts on what I think he should have done.

I've never, ever tried to change his technique but I feel I have stopped him from making rash decisions. At the end of the day, no-one cares a jot about goalkeepers, only goalkeepers care about themselves.

I try and get defenders to think like goalkeepers and I try and get the goalkeeper to think like a defender. You then get that togetherness. I say little things to Tommy, like when someone's crossing the ball.

Last season he was making his mind up whether to come out for the ball before it was even kicked, so this season we worked on waiting until he's picked up the flight of the ball before making a decision. Little things like that have improved his game no end.

During the season, there were plenty of times when he was virtually unemployed in games but, out of the blue, he's had to pull off a magnificent save to keep the points. That's very difficult if your concentration levels are not the greatest, so we work on that aspect.

I tell defenders after a game, in a psychological kind of a way, if the 'keeper's had to make too many saves, telling them if they get in the blocks and stop the crosses to make life easier for Tommy, he'll respond and make life easier for them with some of those last-gasp saves.

He's got the ability to go all of the way, it's just a pity he's not a couple of inches taller, because if he was he'd be a £2m keeper. His kicking has improved, his overall game's improved and my 'keeper's in the PFA Team of the Year and is the club's Player of the Year twice, it all looks good on my CV! It's great to read that he says he owes a lot to Mark Crossley. That is pretty good, still second best to playing though, but pretty rewarding nevertheless.

I know I was understudy to Tommy for a while but really, deep down, we all knew I wasn't going to play, so Tommy knew he was going to play every week. But it came as a shock to his system when I came in for a few games around Christmas time and he came back better for it, keeping three clean sheets in his next four games. I knew I was past my best, but those few games could well be the reason why Tommy Lee is such a good goalkeeper now, so it's vital we have someone to push him as hard as possible.

Now it's all eyes on our prize, 46 games in League One. We've got the go-ahead for some decent recruitment, the new training ground has got the green light so this club has not just gone up a notch, it's jumped up two or three levels.

That's what we've now got to sustain. Being up a level, having a great pitch and playing super football, together with a new training facility, plenty of clubs are starting to ring us offering loan players.

Because we brought on Jack Hunt so well, Lee Clark at Huddersfield is ringing me up saying: "If you need any loan players, let me know." That word will spread round and our 'phone will keep ringing.

We had Donal McDermott here last season. We tried desperately hard to get him back, time and time and time again, but we weren't successful. But when he was here I used to do reports on him saying how he was training, how he was playing, how he was fitting in to the dressing room, how he was behaving. He was a well-mannered young man, a pleasure to have here.

I'd send those reports plus some DVD's off to Manchester City and they felt we were really looking after him. Little things like that help make those great strides forward. Those little things, like the manager always says, turn into big things.

We're striving for at least a top-ten finish next season and, deep down, we'll be disappointed if we miss out. We need to continue wheeling and dealing, there are some big teams with big budgets in League One.

But we hope the supporters have confidence in our ability that we'll do our jobs, bring in the right players to add to what we've already got. Bournemouth and Rochdale have shown the way, now we want to follow their lead. You have to give credit to the chairman, Barrie Hubbard, and to Dave Allen, who owns Sheffield dog track, as well as casinos, and his investment has helped us make giant strides.

The chairman pulled off a great signing when he persuaded Mr Allen to jump on board. He was the one who wanted to bring John sheridan in. The rest is history....

I've learned a lot this season but, by far, the biggest thing is to keep your feet on the ground and never take anything for granted, even though the three of us have just signed new four-year contracts.

It's all a learning curve and I'm learning all of the time and I'm loving it. Having a Championship on my CV is terrific at such an early part of my coaching career.

As for the boss, people think he shouts a lot and that he's on at the players too much, but all that is just his way. He's passionate and he wants to do well and he wants the players to do well.

He doesn't want Chesterfield in the bottom league, it's not acceptable to any of us. We want the players to want what we want. I want to be a top coach and eventually a top manager so learning from people like John Sheridan and others is fantastic. I'm taking notes and I believe that one day, all of that will happen. I want it, I need it and I expect it!

We made it at last, Chesterfield are up as champions

Steady on Tommy Lee! We are close, but not that close

The pressure is off and we can finally celebrate promotion

It's party time after the Gillingham game

I sign a new deal watched by chief executive Carol Wilby

The management team with chairman Barrie Hubbard

Prize possessions - my England U-21 and Wales caps

CHAPTER FIFTEEN
A welcome in the hillside

In 1995 I was playing the best football of my career with Nottingham Forest and I was desperate to test myself on the international stage. It was a big year for me as I was negotiating a new four-year contract with Frank Clark and I was under pressure to choose which country I would play for.

I was confident I was good enough – plus there was a clause in my contract that I got an extra £25,000 if I won a full international cap. I had played three games for England U-21's in 1990 – against Poland, USSR and Czechoslovakia – and would have loved to have played for the senior side. Stuart Pearce said Terry Venables had been asking about me, but the call never came, not even for the 'B' squad. Venables had put his faith in the likes of David Seaman, Tim Flowers, Ian Walker and Nigel Martin. David James was also coming through at Liverpool.

All was not lost though, as I found out I qualified for both Scotland and Wales through my grandparents. I even posed for pictures holding a haggis hoping the publicity might kick-start interest from England. But it never came and I had to eat a big slice of humble pie. But at least I didn't have to eat the haggis!

I found out I qualified for Scotland because my grandmother was born in Edinburgh. I had a lot of calls from journalists in Scotland asking what I was going to do.

Craig Brown was interested in playing me in the 'B' team against Denmark, but Scotland already had two experienced goalkeepers in Alan Rough and the much-maligned Jim Leighton, who was 37 at the time. I'd have been very proud to play for Scotland, but I was already getting stick from Stuart Pearce, who was calling me McCrossley at every opportunity.

I felt I was playing as well as at any time in my career after helping Forest out of the First Division and to third spot in the Premiership in successive seasons and also doing well in European games. The 'C' words consistency and concentration were not always synonymous with me, but I worked hard during the week and fought off the challenge of Northern Ireland international Tommy Wright, but then it all became a bit messy.

Scotland said I wasn't eligible because I had played for England U-21, while the FA said it was OK and gave me the go ahead. But Frank Clark got a bit shirty with me. He didn't want me to play for either Scotland or Wales, because I would then become the club's third assimilated player behind David Phillips and Scott Gemmill.

Clubs were only allowed to play two assimilated players in Europe. Frank was convinced I had what it took to play for England and said that if I played for Scotland he would hit me in the wallet. I'd only get extra cash if I played for England. I was desperate to play for England, but how long was I supposed to wait? Tim Flowers was out of form at Blackburn and with all due respect to Ian Walker, I didn't think he was as good as me. I wanted to test myself in international football against the best in the world. But if England didn't want me then I'd have to look elsewhere.

Then Bobby Gould called out of the blue and asked me to play for Wales. I think I had been recommended by Dean Saunders. I jumped the gun, probably too quickly, although I usually went with my gut feeling and did things on the spur of the moment. Bobby was looking for an understudy to Neville Southall ahead of the World Cup finals in France in 1998. My two rival 'keepers, Forest's Andy Marriott and Notts County's Darren Ward, had already been included in the national squads. I had to send in a lot of things –my grandfather's birth certificate, marriage certificate, my mother's birth certificate, then mine. But, lets face it, if Vinnie Jones was Welsh, then so was I. Like me, Andy had also played for England U-21's before moving to Wrexham for £200,000.

I was happy to turn out for Wales, because it offered me the chance to play with the likes of Mark Hughes, Ryan Giggs, Dean Saunders, Gary Speed, Chris Coleman, John Hartson and Robbie Savage. Now I can't claim for one second that I considered myself to be Welsh. That would be a lie. Had I won 50 caps instead of just the eight I might have felt different. But I was proud, very proud, every time I pulled on that jersey. And I can promise the fans that I always gave 100%.

Playing at the Millenium Stadium for Wales in 2000 was great. It's state of the art; fantastic. The best I've played in. It was a great experience. And to captain the 'B' team was a great honour. But that could have gone better because we played against Scotland at Clyde and lost 4-0. They had a really strong side out, while we fielded a lot of young players and were no match for them. When I first came onto the international scene with Wales, I was understandably very nervous. We had to meet up at the hotel the day before. We had a good night out with a few beers – the manager didn't mind because it helped team bonding.

I was an international virgin and I didn't know a soul, but Vinnie Jones was great. He called me over to join in a game of pool with John Hartson. After that he said we were the Three Amigos, the Three Musketeers.

It was a laugh a minute with Wales and that's important in any dressing room. The last thing you want to see is players sitting there, white as a sheet before a game.

You want to see them with a smile on their face so they can go out and enjoy themselves. And we certainly enjoyed ourselves on trips with Wales. We were away for ten days when we had games on the Saturday and Wednesday – which left plenty of time for partying. Even that wasn't enough for some of the lads. We used to meet up on the Monday, but we would book ourselves into the hotel the day before, go for a game of golf and then go out on the lash. After a meal we would chill out playing carpet bowls in the corridor or table tennis.

We also liked a good old sing-song. Rob Page is a good singer and Gary Speed and Chris Coleman were brilliant on the guitar. We never got bored. After the match we couldn't wait to get changed and get into town for a few beers. Apart from Ryan Giggs, that is. He couldn't show his face because he'd just get mobbed. It was like going to town with Take That!

On one trip, I shared a room with 'keeper Danny Coyne. I'd had a few drinks too many, just to be sociable of course, and when I got back to the room he was asleep. Unfortunately, in my drunken state, I mistook his bed for the loo and started to pee all over him. So much for team bonding!

But that wasn't my most embarrassing experience. We were in Italy with Wales, staying in a hotel with an 'L' shaped pool. My room looked out onto the pool. I had just got out the shower and the lads were by the pool so I went to the window and dropped the towel and did my party piece.

I stood there naked and started acting around until I heard someone shout: "Mark Crossley put it away. See me later." It was the manager, Bobby Gould, who happened to be standing at the window opposite my room.

I thought I was for the high jump. I was sure to get sent home. What would the papers say? More to the point, what would Forest and my mum and dad say? Fortunately, he made a joke of it and let me off with a warning. Fair play to him for that.

Now Bobby Gould loved a meeting. He would call a meeting about having a meeting. He was also keen on videos, he would even video training sessions and play them back to us. He called us in one day to go over a tape and there was Dean Saunders, who was injured at the time, doing a dance behind his back. It was hilarious. On another occasion he put a tape in and it just showed the Brazilian team sitting down to have dinner.

Bobby said we should try to be like them – apparently they all turned up on time, dressed the same and ate the same meal. "If it's good enough for Brazil it's good enough for Wales," he announced. Actually, he had a point. We were bit like the Ragged Arse Rovers at times and it certainly wouldn't have hurt us to be a bit more organised. So what happened next? We went outside to go training and the coach turned up 20 minutes late! So much for being more professional!

One day in training Bobby called us all into a circle and stood in the middle and then did something rather stupid. He called John Hartson into the middle and told him to take his frustration out on him. Now big John is the wrong man to cross. He could have killed Bobby, but he contented himself with kneeling on his chest and ruffling his hair.

Once Bobby dropped Robbie Savage ahead of a game with Italy. Sav had been set up by the Press who persuaded him to be photographed throwing a replica of Paola Maldini's shirt into a bin. But the lads got together and campaigned to have Sav reinstated the next day. He went on to win 39 caps for Wales, until John Toshack took over. Typically all Sav would say was: "John Toshack said my way or the highway – well I'm on the M56."

On another occasion Bobby called Mark Hughes over and told him he was making him captain. Mark said he was honoured, but hadn't he better clear it with the current skipper, Gary Speed, first? So Bobby shouted Gary over and told him he was making Mark skipper. Gary told him, in no uncertain terms, to think again. He was skipper and he was staying skipper – the captaincy of Wales wasn't like confetti, you couldn't just throw it around. Quick as a flash Bobby called Mark back and said: "I've just got the reaction I wanted from Gary and I'm going to stick with him as skipper." Quality.

Later Bobby made Vinnie skipper. He left it to the players to vote and most of them went for Gary Speed or Dean Saunders. But Bobby said he had totted the votes up and it was Vinnie who won. All the lads knew that wasn't true. What the method in that little piece of madness was only Bobby knows.

In the end Bobby said he had taken Wales as far as he could. He was right, he had taken us a long way – from 55th in the world to about 155th! Don't get me wrong. I love the bloke. But, at the end of the day he had probably tried too hard. If that's possible.

I actually felt a little sorry for Bobby because it was an absolute nightmare for him. He tried hard and put his heart and soul into it, but Wales had some big players at the time like Dean Saunders, Mark Hughes, Ryan Giggs and Vinnie Jones. You have to be mentally strong sometimes to handle players of that calibre.

The lads used to call Bobby Gould the wolf because of his thick eyebrows. He thought it was because he was cunning. No, it was the eyebrows Bobby! It really was!

One day, on a trip to Holland, he decided we were going to play charades. So we all got together and decided to play a trick on Bobby. Gareth Hall bounced a ball around pretending to be basketball player and someone shouted 'Teen Wolf'. Poor Bobby didn't realise it was directed at him – and all planned.

Dean Saunders did Michael Jackson's Thriller and everyone, apart from Bobby, was in hysterics by now. Bobby got up to do his little piece but and before he even started someone shouted 'An American Werewolf in London'. It was hilarious.

Dean couldn't resist making fun of Bobby. We had all gone out for a drink and a meal one night when Dean told us all to gather round in a circle. Bobby was buzzing because we'd invited him along and felt part of it.

Dean started to tell a joke about three surgeons, discussing their most successful operations. The first surgeon said he got to the scene of a car crash and found a man who had lost an arm. He put the arm in a bucket of ice, took the man to hospital and sewed it back on. The man recovered well and became a javelin thrower in the GB Olympic team. Surgeon No.2 said he went to a car crash and found a man whose leg had been chopped off at the hip. He put it in ice and sewed it back on in hospital. The operation was such a success than he was now running the 110m hurdles for the GB athletics team.

The third surgeon said that was nothing compared to what he did. A man was taking a sheet of glass off the back of a van when it slipped and sliced his head off. The head rolled into a field of cabbages. They couldn't find the head, so he sewed a cabbage on instead and the man lived. The operation was such a success that he is now managing the Welsh football team.

Bobby Gould laughed his head off and Mark Hughes laughed so much that he fell off his chair. Could you imagine England players doing that to their manager? It just showed the spirit we had. We were more like a club team.

It was great to be part of the international set-up. Mind you I wondered what I had let myself in for when we took on Holland in Eindhoven. I knew I wasn't going to play, I was just there to get to know the squad and act as cover for Neville Southall.

But I was glad I wasn't playing as Dennis Bergkamp and co humiliated our boys 7-1. And poor old Nev was man of the match at that! The Dutch were superb that night, putting 20-30 passes together. The balls they were using were like beach balls; they were flying all over the place. It was almost impossible to keep track of them.

I had never seen anything like it. Ronald de Boer was drilling corners into the box and Bergkamp was volleying them towards goal from every angle. We scored a beauty, but Bergkamp bagged a hat-trick.

I was happy to be understudy to Neville because he was one of the all-time greats for his country, after all he was capped a record 93 times.

Over a period of 15 years he was up there with the best in the world. He seemed to get better every year. People say that 'keepers mature with age and he was living proof of that. I was eager to learn from him at training sessions, but I have to say he didn't do much to help me. He was always having a go at me and, I must admit, being a new boy it made me feel uncomfortable. I found him hard work and it was a bit awkward to say the least.

At the end of the day, I didn't really take to him, which isn't like me. He used to eat meals in his room on his own, which I thought was a bit odd. But not as odd as they day he turned up for training with half his beard shaved off. Mark Pembridge asked him what the fuck was going on and he said he did it just to see how long it took someone to notice.

Once, at Everton, he went into a massive sulk when they went 3-0 down to Leeds. At half-time he refused to go in to the changing rooms and sat down against a goal post. But he was a superb goalkeeper. Sometimes, in training, he would decide he wasn't going to use his hands. He would beat shots away with his elbows and arms and would even dive and head them away. Sometimes he would catch shots one-handed, he was that good.

I finally made my debut in February 1997, against Mick McCarthy's Republic of Ireland side at Cardiff Arms Park, and got Man of the Match. Bobby Gould was forced to play a weakened side and the weather kept the crowd down to just 7,000.

But I didn't care. I was on the big stage now – even if it was normally a ground used for rugby. I made a couple of good stops from Tony Cascarino, Jason McAteer and John Goodman. The rain poured down and the ball was shooting all over the place, but I managed to keep a clean sheet.

Sadly, my international career was almost over before it began and I ended up making only eight appearances after I injured myself in a pre-season game in Finland with Forest.

I just slipped taking a goalkick and ended up on my backside. The lads all thought it was hilarious and fell about laughing. But it was no laughing matter. I knew straight away that I had done some damage. I'll never forget that moment.

The surgeon gave me two options, an operation or a long rest period. I talked it over with my family and decided to give the knife a wide berth. Forest were, as usual, great, and backed my decision to the hilt. They never put any pressure on me to play.

Luckily, I was on a four-year contract and still got paid, but it was a real nightmare, I can tell you. I was in terrible pain and there were times when I thought I wouldn't play again.

I spent six weeks in bed watching daytime television and became addicted to Oprah. On the bright side, my daughter Lilli has just been born and I got to spend time with her. If she saved my sanity it was a lady physio at The Park who saved my career. I went to see her every day except Sunday. It was hard but it was worth it in the end because I had no more trouble with my back for almost ten years.

I finally got back in the international picture against Switzerland in Zurich, ironically when Paul Jones injured his back. I went on for the second half at 0-1 down and almost gave a goal away. I tried to be too clever, reading a free-kick from their striker, who changed his mind at the last minute and swerved it the opposite way. Fortunately, it flew just wide. I'd have looked a right prat if that one had gone in.

With Bobby gone and Mark Hughes now at the helm, I came on for the second half against Argentina and kept a clean sheet again. Even though it was only a friendly there was a full house of 70,000. When I saw their team I thought "Fucking hell, what am I doing here?"

In the match against Germany, I left team-mate Robert Page seeing stars. I spotted a one-on-one up front and launched the ball. Unfortunately, Rob was in the way and it cleaned him out. I kicked the ball so hard that it re-bounded off him and only just cleared the bar as it went for a corner. I was praying: "Get over the bar you bastard." After all there were only 75,000 in the crowd watching me! But I played really well and made a good save before Rob Earnshaw put the only goal past Oliver Khan. It was the second time I had knocked someone out. In a game against Wimbledon, I gathered a corner and looked to get it away quickly. I caught the ball so sweetly. Unfortunately it also caught the referee on the head and knocked him out. In those days Saint & Greavsie (remember them?) gave out mugs for players who did something unusual and I was presented with one.

I was disappointed to miss out playing against the great Brazilians like Roberto Carlos. I assumed I would be playing because Paul Jones was injured, but an hour before the game Mark Hughes announced that Roger Freestone was playing and I was sub. I was devastated, absolutely gutted that I never got on. Roger is a great guy but he wasn't a great keeper. But I wasn't even in the 'Boro team at the time, so I suppose I couldn't complain too much. And, after all, Roger was Welsh!

Mark told me I was still a valued member of the squad and that he wanted me around for what I brought to the dressing room. To be honest, there were a few 'boring' lads on the scene at the time and I used to try and spice things up.

When John Toshack took over from Mark Hughes he rang me and said he was picking me in his next squad, along with Danny Coyne. He was starting to look to the future but I was 37 and I couldn't see myself figuring in the future.

I had just gone through a bad divorce and my mind was all over the place. It would have been nice to get away from my poxy flat, which was becoming like a prison, but the last thing I was thinking about was football.

I didn't want to go out and play in the wrong frame of mind and let the lads, and the country, down. So I said: "I'm announcing my international retirement now." I added that if they were short one day, then I was only a 'phone call away. But that call never came....

Playing for Wales against the Republic of Ireland in 1997

The Welsh team that played Scotland in 2004

A tense moment as I line up for Wales alongside Ryan Giggs and future manager Gary Speed

I was so proud every time I pulled on that international jersey

I meet up with my mate Mark Williams before the international with the Republic of Ireland

I'm not feeling myself today. Not sure how I got talked into this....

CHAPTER SIXTEEN
The long arm of the law

I was a bit of a wild child I suppose and trouble has followed me around in the past. Maybe I got in with the wrong people. But I really made a mess of things the time I ended up in a cell after a night out on the town with my mates. We were waiting to be picked up and I was just messing about with my cousin. He lost his balance and as I tried to catch him I smashed a window in an empty shop.

It's not true that a brick was thrown at the window. It was a pure accident, but it was captured on CCTV and the police became involved. The upshot was I was held in a police cell at two in the morning while they looked at the footage. They let me out at 5am with a caution on the understanding I paid the £450 damages, which wasn't a problem.

Unfortunately, we had a big FA Cup match at Portsmouth on the Saturday and I drove straight to the ground for training, although I was probably still well over the limit. I never said a word to anyone as we set off on the overnight trip to Portsmouth, but it was eating away at me and I was bricking myself at the back of the bus. I was so upset that I went to Stuart Pearce and asked him what to do. He told me to go and see the gaffer because it would be all over the Sunday papers the following morning.

There was a curtain half way down the bus. The gaffer had his back to me, so I just stood there and waited. After a while I zipped the curtain back up and went back to my seat. I said I had told the gaffer, but I never did. I just couldn't bring myself do it, I didn't have the bottle. Unfortunately, the press were already on to it, and the telephone calls soon started. In the first minute of the cup tie I dropped a cross and the ball was tapped into the net.

Forest fans behind the goal were pelting me with coins in the second half and I spent the rest of the game praying that we would win. I just couldn't concentrate on the match. The next morning I was up at 5am and went round to the paper shop. The papers were tied up in a bundle on the pavement and sure enough there was the back page headline screaming up at me. "Crossley clanger follows night in the slammer."

Brian Clough rang my dad, but it was me who answered the telephone. "It's your gaffer, put your father on," said Cloughie. My dad thought it was someone messing about, but soon realised it wasn't when Cloughie laid into him. He blamed my dad for letting me out on the town on a Thursday night, but my dad rightly said that he couldn't keep an eye on me 24/7. Cloughie told me to report to the ground the following day.

He was waiting at the gate and said: "I'm not sure whether to sack you or not. Go and get a drink while I think about what I am going to do". Wisely, I let my dad take the flak and just sat there, quiet as a mouse. In the end Clough said: "I'm fining you two weeks wages, suspending you for two weeks and playing young Marriott. And if he does well, you won't be playing in the League Cup final against Manchester United".

I was gutted, but then Liam O'Kane told me that the boss was thinking of playing me. He had to play me didn't he? After all, I had played in every game up to the final and had been in superb form. But he left me out. There couldn't have been a worse punishment. The gaffer brought me back for the next game. He had made his point. I didn't blame him. I let both myself and the club down. He gave me my big break in the game and I let him down. The punishment was right and fair, but the real punishment was missing out on the Wembley final.

Cloughie gave me two weeks to find somewhere to live in Nottingham and I bought Steve Chettle's house in Bilborough. Luckily he wanted a quick sale. But I got my fingers burned with that one, literally. I was on a pre-season tour to Sweden when

Alan Hill told me there had been a fire at the house. I had left Steve Guinan and Lee Stratford house-sitting while I was away and it almost burnt down. Hilly said I could go home if I wanted, but I thought "What's the point?" I went to live with a mate round the corner while the insurance company sorted the mess out.

I reached another crossroads in my life in 1993. Brian Clough had retired by now and Forest appointed Frank Clark as manager. It was in the summer when I ended up in court, facing a long stretch in prison.

It all kicked off when I was attacked in Barnsley. I'd been out for a few drinks with my girlfriend at the time, Hayley Skelton. We stopped off for some fish and chips when a lad walked up and deliberately knocked them out of her hand. Instinctively, I stepped in and gave him a slap.

As far as I was concerned that was the end of it. But, as we walked back to her parents' house I got the feeling we weren't alone. The next minute eight guys were on top of me, beating me up. I got a really good hiding and had about fifty bite marks on my back, some of which broke the skin. I managed to break free and we ran off.

My face was black and blue, I could have been killed, so I went to the police and one lad was arrested. I wanted to press charges, but the police advised me that it would be better to let the matter drop before the papers got hold of the story. They said the lad would only get a slap on the wrists at the end of the day anyway, I recognised one of the gang, a big lad who worked locally as a doorman.

When I bumped into him in a pub a few weeks later I went over and asked him why he got involved and he tried to make out he was just trying to help me, which was rubbish.

I should have let sleeping dogs lie, I suppose. But I kept hearing talk that he was out to get me. It started playing on my mind, so I found out where he lived and went round there with my cousin. To this day I don't know what possessed me to go round there. I just wanted to chat and sort things out. I didn't want it to fester and thought it was time to clear the air. But he got the wrong idea and came running out and hit me on the back, with a baseball bat I think. It all kicked off then with my cousin wading in to to save me and the guy fell on a broken milk bottle and ended up in hospital.

I went to my girlfriend's house and my cousin went home. The next minute there were six police cars outside the door and I was arrested and banged up for three days. The police were charging us with attempted murder and we were told that we could be looking at five years in prison.

But I hadn't done anything, I hadn't touched him. My parents were distraught. My mum couldn't even face me. She was livid, but she didn't know the full story. My barrister assured me that justice would be done, but it was 18 months of sheer hell as the case dragged on. I had a few sleepless nights, I can tell you.

I was worried to death because it would have been the end of my career at Forest. Ironically, I had just had a great season. When it finally went to court the charges were dropped to GBH with intent. Fortunately for us the lad told lies in court. He claimed he wasn't armed, but the forensic evidence told a different story. The mark on my back had clearly been caused by a baseball bat or something like a cricket stump.

It was also confirmed that I hadn't been involved in the fight because I didn't have a speck of blood on me. In the end, I got a suspended sentence and a £1,500 fine. I was also ordered to pay £750 compensation. My cousin, Andy, went down for a year and served six months.

Andy and me had always been close as kids; he was like a brother to me. But we fell out over this and it caused a big rift among the two families. But we made up in later years and I was best man at his wedding. There was talk that I had paid him to take the rap for me. That's not true. But I did agree to look after his family while he was inside, which was only right and proper, because he only got involved in the first place to protect me. We both got off lightly I suppose. After that I realised that I had to get my life sorted out and quickly.

The other occasion when I fell foul of the long arm of the law just started out as a bit of fun. I left a spoof message, in a funny accent, on my answer phone for my mum and dad. I'd got a few videos out that were overdue and the lady from the shop 'phoned when I was out.

For some reason she took exception to the message. She said it was racist and that she would be calling the police. I didn't pay much attention until there was a knock on the door one night and I opened it to find two policemen standing there.

Now, no way am I a racist, one of my friends is Zesh Rehman, who used to play for Pakistan and Fulham. It was just a bit of fun. The police told me to play the tape and one of them was pissing himself with laughter.

The other, also struggling to keep a straight face, just told me to wipe the tape and make sure I didn't do anything like it again. Unfortunately, I still had to return the videos. I didn't fancy getting a bollocking from the angry lady, so I sat outside the shop until it closed at ten at night and posted them through the letterbox. I never went back again.

That wasn't quite as bad as when Larry Lloyd, John Robertson and myself joined Brian Clough on stage for a Q&A session in Nottingham. The place was packed and there were about 1,000 in the audience when a chap, in a turban, stood up to ask a question. But, before he could say anything, BC said: "Hold on a minute son, have you banged your head?"

The chap said "No" and Cloughie replied: "Why have you got a bandage on your head then? I'm only joking, carry on. What's your question son?" Only Brian Clough could get away with that. But it wasn't racist; he was only having a laugh. And the chap with the bandage on his head had a right laugh too....

New baby Alfie with Emma ....they are the future!

CHAPTER SEVENTEEN
Love, Marriage and Divorce

I used to love going to the Black Orchid nightclub, in Nottingham, on a Monday night. As a single man and a Forest player, there was no shortage of young ladies wanting to get to know you, especially after a few drinks.

Sex was being offered on a plate and I was never one to turn down a meal. I ate pretty well in those days, I can tell you! Can you blame me? After all, you are only young once.

I used to go to the Orchid with Nigel Jemson, who was a bit of a smoothie. We used to go in the VIP area and girls were throwing themselves at us.

After a night at the Orchid we would go to see Sally Reacher (the daughter of the Forest chairman) who had a pub in Nottingham and we'd stay there until four or five in the morning. She was a right party girl and we had some great nights there. I also liked a night out in Derby at the Pink Coconut but, being a Forest player, I got too much grief. The only other option was London, but trips down there were a rarity.

Often Jemmo and me would go out with the same girl. It didn't really matter, there were plenty to go around and I had a lot of one-night stands and played the field. I rarely took any precautions, which was stupid.

When I was at Fulham, I ended up in hospital after warts appeared on an intimate area. I went to a clinic in Harley Street and booked in under the name of Bill Smith.

They called for Bill Smith to come to report to the desk several times, but I sat there like a lemon for about five minutes until a nurse came out and I realised they were shouting me. Fortunately, it wasn't a big problem and I was told they could have been dormant for years.

I was big on holiday romances and I started going out with a girl from Liverpool, who I met during a foam party in Kaves. I took her to the Orchid for a night out, but several girls who I knew kept coming up and talking to me. She wasn't too happy, but I didn't pay too much attention to it.

The lass certainly got my attention later that night, that's for certain. I was asleep in bed when she hit me on top of the head with a big wooden statue! It had a heavy wooden base and left me with a massive lump on my head. It could have killed me.

Needless to say, that was the last I saw of her. Unfortunately, I had bought her a car as a present, a Peugeot 306, so I gave my dad the spare key and said he could have it if he went down to Liverpool to collect it.

I also met my wife, Gaynor Mann, on holiday in Malia in Crete. I was asked to go with a bunch of lads when someone pulled out at the last minute. All I had to pay was the air fare. I wasn't doing anything so I thought "Sod it, why not?" She was there with four mates. We got chatting on the plane and we all had a right laugh.

She told me she had a boyfriend who was a Forest fan, but said it wasn't serious. Fancy going all that way and meeting a lass from Nottingham! I thought it would just be a holiday romance, but we soon got together back home. It was fate I suppose.

But it turned out to be the most expensive holiday I ever had because it ended up costing me close to a million pounds when we got divorced. But at least we had our two gorgeous kids, Lilli and Tommy, to show for it.

I married Gaynor in Plumtree, she was 21 and I was 28. We took a cruise around the Caribbean and visited St Lucia on the honeymoon.

The press were all over us when we got together and her ex-boyfriend accused me of stealing his girlfriend. It got worse after we were married. One night I got home to find a message on my answer phone, allegedly from The Sun newspaper.

They said they had incriminating evidence of me with a young lady in the manager's office at the Orchid and would I ring them back. But I knew it wasn't true, because I'd never set foot in the manager's office. Needless to say, I didn't call them back and I never heard any more about it. Perhaps an old girl-friend had tried to sell them a 'Kiss and Tell' story? Perhaps it was a wind-up? I never did find out.

We had a smashing house in a quiet cul-de-sac in Edwalton. One day a letter, with no stamp on it, was pushed through the letterbox. It was addressed to Gaynor and stated that I had been having an affair for some time and that the lads had been with two strippers in the toilets at the club's Christmas party.

Gaynor was in tears but I told her it was a load of rubbish. I never did find out who sent the letter, but I do know that it was a rotten thing to do. The sad thing is that it may have been someone who knew us well, how else did they know the address? Neighbours reported seeing a red car outside the house but, apart from that, there were no other clues.

I'd had a few late nights with the lads. One night I'd been drinking in Faces, a bar in Nottingham, and lost track of the time. I didn't get in until about four in the morning and crept in to find her sitting in a chair, crying her eyes out. She demanded to know where I'd been and thought I'd been with another woman. I hadn't. But for some reason I panicked.

I said I'd been caught having a pee in an alley and taken to Canning Circus police station. She said: "What was the name of the policeman?" I don't know how it came to me, but I suddenly blurted out "PC Harold."

The next day I was shopping in Asda when Gaynor tele-phoned, in tears again, calling me a lying bastard. She'd only called the police station and found out there was no PC Harold. I'd been caught red-handed. But the ironic thing was, I really hadn't done anything wrong.

Things weren't good at home and she told me she had been with her dad to see a solicitor about how she stood if we ever split up. I didn't believe her. But, a few years later, at Middlesbrough, I realised it must have been true. I thought a move to London would improve out relationship. How wrong could I be? We only lasted 12 months. When I was at Fulham, I received a letter from Gaynor's solicitors filing for divorce.

Even after I got the letter, I still believed we could work things out, if only for our two lovely children.

I still liked a night out with the lads and if I wasn't back by 2am I would find myself locked out and sleeping in the Wendy house. The kids thought it was funny when they came down for breakfast to find their dad, in a suit and tie, curled up in there.

I wanted to go to marriage guidance for the sake of the kids, but Gaynor would not have it. She is a tough little cookie and had already made her mind up that it was over between us. I think she regrets it now, but I've moved on.

One day she left and took the kids back to her parent's house in Nottingham. Then it began to hit home that I really was about to lose her. She said that there wasn't anyone else. But I had my suspicions after I found a text from a man on her 'phone saying "Have I told you lately?"

To be honest, I wasn't too worried about that. The only thing that was eating away at me was that she had become ruthless and had even gone as far as dividing the fridge into two, with tape and arrows. One night I came home and there was nothing to eat on my side so I helped myself to a couple of chicken legs from her side. But she caught me eating them and knocked them out of my hand.

I was worried about losing the kids, along with the house and everything else. Over the next few days I started to crack up and even became suicidal. I couldn't see a light at the end of the tunnel. I wasn't sleeping very well and I was spaced out.

Chris Coleman came to see me, which was good of him, but

to this day I can't remember a word of the conversation.

Without the support of Chris and my parents, I don't know what I would have done. At my lowest point, I remember getting all the tablets out of the medicine cupboard and lining them up on the kitchen table.

One day, I'd been drinking and woke up at five in the morning, freezing outside my back door. I was curled up in the corner by the fence with a kitchen knife in my hand. I hadn't taken any tablets, but I was ashamed of myself.

How could I sink so low as to even think about taking my own life? How could I be so selfish to even consider leaving Lilli and Tommy? But I suppose that is where I was at.

Somehow, I managed to pull myself together. I started to train harder to take my mind of things for a while and got myself really fit. Then my parents, Watt Nicoll, Nigel Jemson and other close friends, like Mark Williams, helped me to pull through.

When we split up, Fulham had just offered me a new deal, but Leeds wanted me as well. I asked Gaynor if she planned to move back to Nottingham because, if she was, I would sign for Leeds so that I could be close to the kids. It made common-sense, but I was banging my head against a brick wall.

I wasn't a saint by any means, but I wasn't a bad husband either. I came from a close family and my marriage meant a lot to me. I love my kids and get them for half the school holidays. When we have a game in the area I get to stay with them and we keep in touch on Facebook and the webcam.

We have a great relationship considering that I'm so far away from them. I miss them of course and if I don't see them for two or three weeks it starts to get to me. It hurts. Six years down the line, it doesn't get any easier, because I've missed a big part of them growing up.

The law as it stands stinks. Fathers should have equal rights in a divorce, but they don't. I'm a brilliant dad and make a 500-mile round trip just to see them. But if Gaynor suddenly says I can't see the kids that day, what can I do about it? Nothing! Gaynor is a very good mum, don't get me wrong, but she made life very difficult for me during our divorce. It cost me £100,000 on legal fees alone. It was £100 every time the solicitors sent me a letter and I ended up paying her a £600,000 lump sum and 37% of my income in maintenance. It is 20% for the kids and 17% to her, which I'm still paying.

Why? Obviously I'm happy to look after my kids, but why should I have to keep paying her to live in London? She divorced me remember. It's her choice to stay in London. She has a job teaching at Tommy's school and has a new partner, while I've got a new family to look after now as well. Surely that should be taken into account? It's all wrong.

We are supposed to live in a society of equal rights. But this is very unequal as far as I am concerned. I stopped the maintenace once when she stopped me seeing the kids and world war three broke out and I almost ended up in court again. It upset Lilli and I don't want that to happen again.

It was very bitter at the time. I still am, because I don't know what went wrong. I went away with Fulham on an end-of-season trip and she suddenly said: "If you go, when you get back there'll be a letter waiting for you"

It broke my heart you know; it really did. I hoped that I'd get her back one day, but it wasn't to be. Kids can put a strain on any marriage, but it wasn't their fault. I suppose we just fell out of love.

We had been together for ten years and had been sleeping in separate bedrooms for a while. But I never dreamed we would get divorced, simply because of Tommy and Lilli.

When I played for Fulham we lived in a six-bedroomed house in Kingswood, which was obviously too big for Gaynor. She wanted me to move out but I refused. Fortunately it sold quite quickly, in about three months, so we weren't under each other's feet for long during the bitter divorce proceedings.

I moved into Louis Boa Morte's flat, which was vacant, but I was having a rough time. I got through a box set of the Sopranos in a month. I was lost. Life was just a blur. I would go swimming, play poker online for hours or 'phone my mum and dad just for someone to talk to.

I was that lonely and depressed. I would find myself just looking out of the kitchen window for hours on end. All I had to look forward to was training and the kids coming round to the flat. I would not wish it on anybody. After my divorce, I ended up hitting the London nightlife constantly with a mate of mine, Zat Knight, who lived around the corner from me. He helped me get through the break-up. Zat had a lot of contacts and on one occasion took me to a premiere in London, to watch the 50 Cent film "Get Rich Or Die Trying". We went to the party afterwards and met 50 Cent. What a night that was!

Obviously, being a single lad again and with the models and that we had a great time. I started having some fun again. We used to get changed out of our match-day suits into jeans in the car in Wimbledon Village and head for London. We'd have a few drinks to warm up and head for a club at about two in the morning. I used to go to a club called Secrets with Zat, Elvis Hammond and Barry Hales. We used to get in for nothing and got lap dances for half the price.

It got to the stage where football was getting in the way of my social life. The drink took my mind off my divorce, but when I woke up the next morning things seemed ten times worse and I got even more depressed. Then Emma came into my life....

Out of the blue I was asked to go on a stag do to Magaluff with Ted Soppitt, who trained my greyhounds.

I had too much to drink on the first day and had a right hang-over. I was getting some water down me when Ted's brother, Steve, introduced me to Emma, who was staying just down the road. It was fate again, I suppose.

I had a walk up the beach the following day and sat with her and her mate, Andrea. We kept in touch after that and she used to drive to Newcastle airport and fly down for the weekend. But she doesn't even like football. In fact, sometimes she wouldn't even come to a game at Fulham, she'd wait for me in the flat. No way is she a WAG, she's brilliant, top drawer and I'm madly in love with her.

The ten-year gap in our ages doesn't bother me. I thought it might be a problem at first, but it's not. I cannot believe how well we get on. She is my best mate and I can't wait to marry her.

I soon realised that I was in love with Emma. The problem was that I had just bought a house in Epsom, not knowing 100% that Fulham were releasing me. But I had decided that I'd had enough of London. Anyway, I wanted to be closer to my family.

My investment in the house was a good one and I ended up renting it out to Mark Williams, who was moving back to the UK after living in Spain for five years. I did a deal with Mark to keep a room in the house for me to stay in when I came back to visit my children.

I met Mark when we were on loan at Stoke. We were staying in the same hotel and became best mates. I was best man at his wedding when he married top glamour girl Linsey Dawn McKenzie. I was a witness at their wedding at the Registry Office in London. We had a few drinks at the Sanderson Hotel in London and it turned out to be a hell of a night. We were joined by Mark Smith (Rhino from the hit television show Gladiators) and his wife. Unfortunately, the other witness, Linsey's mate, Nikki, had too much to drink and fell down some steps. She ended up breaking her nose and was taken to hospital in an ambulance.

Later that year they had a blessing in Spain, where they were living at the time. It was a massive do with Jodie Marsh as matron of honour and me as best man. OK Magazine covered it and I brought the house down with my speech.

The next day we had an all-day pool party. What a wicked party that was as well as it was also their son, Luca's, birthday. Five years later, their wedding was featured on Celebrity Four Weddings and I was best man again. They should have won, but Tina Malone, from the show ''Shameless'', only gave them four out of ten for the meal, which was a surprise, because it was cooked by a Michelin star chef at the El Oceano hotel and was ten times better then hers.

Emma and myself are getting married at El Oceano next June. We've got 40 guests, close family and friends, to share our special day. My son Tommy is best man and Lilli is the chief bridesmaid. It's going to be perfect. When we get back home we are having a big do for everyone.

I've picked the right one this time. Emma is brilliant. She may be younger than me, but I love her to bits. I can't tell you how I felt when she told me that she was pregnant with our son, Alfie.

Lilly and Tommy were also excited at the prospect of having a new brother. They both helped in deciding his name. I was worried about how the new baby would affect them but I needn't have worried as they have both taken to the new addition exceptionally well.

It's a great feeling being a dad again, although I had forgotten about the sleepless nights. Not bad for someone who said he'd never marry again ....or have any more kids for that matter.

I was delighted when I heard that Emma was pregnant with Alfie, as she had miscarried the previous year and was terribly uspet. I can't help but wipe a tear from my eye when I see her stare at little Alfie, who arrived at 12.50pm on Monday, May 23, 2011.

During the labour, we were both concerned when not one, but two consultants kept coming in to check on Alfie's heartbeat. They told us there was a chance Emma would have to have an emergency C-section as the baby was showing signs of distress.

Emma had been in labour for nearly 24 hours, but took it all in her stride.

Ten minutes later they decided to operate and the next thing I knew I was in a set of scrubs sitting next to Emma, holding her hand. Amazingly, it was Emma who was reassuring me.

I felt sick and had my head in my hands. A member of the operating staff came round to talk to me and I couldn't believe my eyes. It was David Bamforth, someone I went to school with, and we started talking about pigeon racing, of all things.

The next thing I knew, Alfie had been born. He was blue when he came out because the umbilical cord had been wrapped around his neck. Thankfully, he is fine now and so is Emma.

I'm so proud to have three lovely kids and all the heartache is going away. Now I just want us all to be happy and healthy in the future....

My Forest team-mates turned out at my wedding to Gaynor

The big day with mum and dad

Best man this time....

That famous pool party in Spain after the wedding of the year

All the fun of the fair at a family outing on the Costa del Sol

A family gathering in Epsom with my mum and the kids

A blast from the past. My old mates at my birthday party

Happier times on holiday with Lilli and Tommy in Portugal

Barnsley's most wanted! At my cousin's wedding

I miss Lilli and Tommy. They are growing up so fast

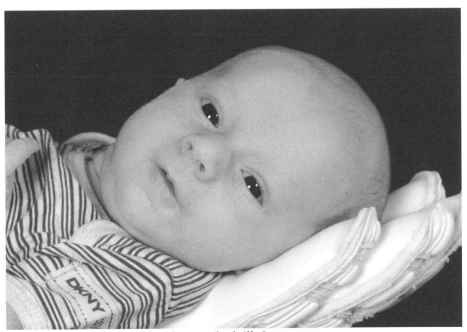

The new arrival, little Alfie who weighed 6lb 9oz

Frank Clark never really got the credit he deserved at Forest

CHAPTER EIGHTEEN
One out of 21 ain't bad

I've played under 21 managers in my long career. And there is only one I couldn't really get along with – David Platt. I think he just used Forest as a stepping stone to get the England job with Sven. But I must admit I might be biased because we never saw eye to eye. The fact is, David Platt forced me to leave Forest, the club I loved. Simple as that.

He said from day one that he had to get rid of the dead wood. And, for some, reason, I knew he meant me. Platt wanted the old pictures of Forest's glory days taking down when he arrived at the City Ground. That was his first mistake. Instead of upsetting people, he should have turned it to his advantage.

He came up to me at the start of the season and said I had until Christmas to prove that I was the No.1 'keeper, which was, I suppose, fair enough. Dave Beasant, who was to coach me later at Fulham, was also at the club. It is strange how the paths of certain players cross throughout their careers.

When he first arrived at the City Ground, Platt signed three Italian players a couple of weeks before the start of the season. That was his second mistake. They weren't match fit and didn't know how we played. The back four ended up deeper than the ocean when we lost 3-0 to Ipswich.

Then, one day he just said to me: "Enough is enough." I hadn't got a clue what he was talking about.

In December 1999 I was left out after turning in disappointing performances against Huddersfield and Tranmere. The manager told me on the training pitch that I was dropped.

When I saw him walking towards me I thought he was coming to discuss a new contract. But it was just the opposite. It was a massive shock as all I wanted to do, at that stage of my career, was to play football. I was confused, but I had been in the situation before. When Platt finally offered me a contract he had cut my pay in half. I loved the club and had been there for a long time. There was no way I wanted to leave, especially in my testimonial year. I loved Nottingham and was happy there. My wife was from Nottingham; my two kids were born there. All things considered, I had a great life in the city. But how could anyone in their right mind expect me to accept that?

I know the board needed to cut the wage bill, but I didn't see why I should be asked to take such a big pay cut. Nevertheless, I told him that I would continue to give 110% whenever I was in the side.

Apparently Stuart Pearce rang from West Ham and asked if I could help them out for a couple of games. But Platt never even told me of their interest. It didn't make any sense. He wanted me out of the club, yet here he was turning down the chance to let me go to West Ham. He said he didn't want to go to Wolves with no recognised 'keeper as cover. To this day, I don't know why David Platt didn't like me. I never slagged him off, even though I could have done plenty of times.

I got back in the side when Dave Beasant was sent off in the 4-3 defeat at Grimsby. But I knew the writing was on the wall the day Dennis Booth gave me a letter saying the contract offer had been withdrawn by the club. It was a blow, but it was no good moaning about it. I just had to get on with life....

Frank Clark

I love Frank Clark. I have the utmost respect for him, as a manager and a man. I had a feeling that he didn't rate me. He never told me, but I could tell. Perhaps it was when he signed Tommy Wright for £450,000 that gave it away. When Frank came in to fill the biggest shoes in football I had just been in trouble with my court case. He thought I was going down – and so did I for that matter. Some people were suprised when he took the job at

Forest, after we were relegated in Brian Clough's final year, but I wasn't. There is an old saying about never going back, but he loved the club and I think it needed an ex-player to get us back on our feet again. It has to be said, he did a cracking job in difficult circumstances. He had won the Fourth Division play-offs with Orient and I don't think he got the credit he deserves.

He bought and sold wisely and got the club promoted. He had around £4m to spend and he spent it well on two top-class strikers – Bryan Roy and Stan Collymore, who only cost £2.2m. And he got us back into Europe. In fact, we were the only English club left playing in Europe at that time.

For the first time we talked about the opposition, which Brian Clough never did. We practised set-pieces and corners.This was a first for us as well and I, for one, liked it. Far from getting rid of me, we got on well and he gave me my first big contract. When Leeds United came in for me we were on holiday in Cala Millor and Frank asked me if I had been tapped up. I hadn't. This was the first I'd heard of it. He told me Leeds had made an offer and that I had permisison to talk to them, but asked me not to sign anything until I'd spoken to him. Leeds offered me £300,000 a year, but I stayed at Forest for less money and Leeds ended up signing Nigel Martin instead.

Tommy Wright was a great goalkeeper, but he had a night-mare start on and off the field. When he got injured, I suddenly got back in the side and played some of the best football of my career. I ended up having a great season and we got promoted. The following year we finished third in the Premiership at the first attempt.

The spirit in the team was great, we'd all go out into town with the girls to celebrate a win. But it all went sour the following season and we went 16 games without a win. I can't explain it, but selling key players like Bryan Roy and Stan Collymore, who joined Liverpool for a record £8.4m, obviously didn't help. Colin Cooper also departed, along with Kevin

Campbell. But that's the nature of football. Players come and go all the time. Frank was big enough to hold his hand up and walk away. He decided he had taken the club as far as he could. He came into the dressing room in tears and resigned there and then. Before long he was named manager at Manchester City.

I got in touch with Frank before I had my interview for the manager's job at Bradford to ask him for advice because this was new territory for me. He just said: "Be yourself big man and you will be fine."

Dave Bassett

I liked 'Harry' Bassett, even though I never got to work with him that much because of injury. Even though he talks too much and too fast. It was strange having a Cockney in Nottingham, you don't see many of them, do you? Dean Saunders does a great impression of him. But, if I ever I want advice, Dave would be one of the first men I would turn to. He's a top guy, but he's also a tough guy. One day, I think it was a game at Huddersfield, Dean was on the wing and had a bit of a go at him. It ended up being Dean's last game at Forest. I'll never forget when we were playing Arsenal at Highbury. I came off my line and Dennis Bergkamp dinked the ball over me.

"You were like a flying pig coming out of goal," said Bassett. "You made his mind up for him."

Apart from that, Harry was great with me and let me go to Millwall on loan to get some games under my belt. It got me going again. I don't think he fancied me at first, but I think I became his best mate the day I clashed with Pierre van Hooij-donk.

Harry was a clever bloke. Clever enough to employ good men like Mike Kelly and Bobby Houghton. He was also top drawer when it came to handling the media.

At one stage, I thought Harry was going to take me to Leicester, but it never happened....

Ron Atkinson

I thought big Ron was great. He was a right laugh and he also hated Pierre van Hooijdonk's guts. I bumped into him on his first day, when he was coming out of the changing rooms before training. He was definitely shocked to see me.

"Shit I didn't know you were still here. Can you still kick a ball a long way?" he asked. "What's going wrong here? Work hard and you will get your chance."

And he was true to his word, putting me in the side after we lost 8-1 to Manchester United and 5-0 to Chelsea.

Big Ron used to like joining in the five-a-sides, he would straddle the halfway line with one foot in each half.

One day he told Pierre to go back to the changing rooms and Pierre told him he could see why he was doing those Carling Black Label adverts on television because he was nothing more than a pub manager.

Ron had a flip chart and went through the opposition team one by one in the hotel before a game. We used to meet up for lunch and then get the coach to the ground. Don't ask me why, it's just the way he liked to do things.

I liked Ron, but he was on a mission impossible at the City Ground. He only had 16 games to avoid relegation. I think he should have been given the job the following year, because I believe he would have got us back up.

Ron had the knack of making you feel ten feet tall, even when you were bottom of the league. He put me in the team and I saved three penalties against Charlton, Sheffield Wednesday and Blackburn, when Steve Chettle was sent off.

By the way, big Ron still has a pair of my golf shoes I loaned him them when he turned up to play in my testimonial golf day. He said: "These are comfy. I'll give them back on Monday." That was about ten years ago. Can I have them back now, please, Ron?

Bryan Robson

Bryan Robson signed me for Middlesbrough of course, but I think a lot of that was down to my old Forest team-mate Colin Cooper. I was poised to sign for Hibs when Colin 'phoned me to see what I was doing. I had made up my mind to try my luck in Scotland. It appealed to me because Hibs weren't a bad side and you got to play Celtic and Rangers four times a year.

I would have been the top earner at the club on £4,000 a week. Plus, Edinburgh is not the worst place in the world to be, is it? But, the next minute, Bryan called and told me not to sign. I knew Viv Anderson and Gordon McQueen were up there with him, so it was an offer I couldn't refuse really. After all, this was Captain Fantastic, a national icon, calling me. I was star-struck just talking to him on the telephone, even though I had played against him in the past.

Sadly, even being a national hero did not help Bryan when it came to management and he did not have the best of times. It was good to have Viv around and I stayed in the same hotel as him for a while. He was always laughing and cracking jokes, but he didn't do much in training, apart from collect the balls and cones. Training was mainly small-sided games, nothing too tactical. I was shocked when I found out he had been treated for throat cancer out in Hong Kong. But he's a fighter and if anyone can beat it, he can.

Terry Venables

When Bryan Robson was struggling to get a win at Middlesbrough, he called his old England boss, Terry Venables, in to help him. Terry had a great reputation in football and was a master tactician. When Bryan got the sack, Terry was left with 16 games to save the club from relegation. We stayed up and he saved the club millions.

I was delighted, especially for chairman Steve Gibson, who put his heart and soul, not to mention millions of pounds, into the club. I was also pleased for the fans. They are fanatical up there and it is sad to see the way the club has declined. They deserve more.

I liked Terry Venables. He liked a laugh and a joke, but he was also a stickler for discipline. He had great qualities in his coaching and management techniques.

There came a time when I wanted some time off, something I had never done before. I'll never forget what he said: "Since I have been here you have been a fantastic pro. I know I can rely on you, even though you have not been in the team. It's not a problem."

He also revealed how close he was to calling me up for England when he was in charge. Those few words meant a lot to me.

Chris Coleman

I knew Chris from playing for Wales and we hit it off straight away. I have a lot of respect for him. He is a bright young manager, a funny guy, a real people person and I can't believe he was out of the game for so long. But he's not a coach. That's why he was wise enough to promote Steve Kean from youth-team coach at Fulham.

Chris was brilliant with me when I was going through my divorce and told me to take as much time off as I needed. He had just been involved in a bad car crash and used to drive round the training ground in a golf buggy.

Basically, he had gone off the road and hit a tree out in the middle of nowhere. He had been trapped alone in the wreck and could hear petrol dripping. He tought he was a goner. But he was rescued and taken to hospital where they took a big chunk of muscle out of his back to repair his mangled leg.

When he showed me his injury I was horrified. There was a massive lump. When I asked what it was he said: "Don't worry, it's just my back." It was horrific. We still keep in touch and I like to play golf with him.

Brian Laws

I can't say he was my best mate at Forest – he knocked about with Gary Parker – but we got on well. He was hard and tough as a player. He tried to sign me when he was manager at Scunthorpe, where he did a brilliant job, but I was not ready to drop down to that level.

When I heard he got a job at Sheffield Wednesday I put a call in to him because I was available for a month on loan. I didn't know he'd already spoken to Dave Beasant and the upshot was that I went up there the very next day. In fact, I was his first signing for The Owls.

Mark Hughes

Mark was at Manchester United when I went up there on loan and I also played against him. I always seemed to play well against Manchester United and never let Wales down, so I thought he might have rated me more. But he put his faith in Paul Jones. Paul was a solid keeper, but I thought I was better.

Mark made the transition from international player to international manager so smoothly and all the players respected him. His attention to detail was first class. When we played Russia I'm sure he could have told us what they had for breakfast if we asked him. He was probably one of the best managers Wales have had and they came within a whisker of qualifying for the European championships under him. We drew 0-0 in Russia, but then lost 1-0 at home in the qualifying play off.

I always thought he would be a good manager in the Premiership and he's slowly proving that, despite being sacked by Manchester City and quitting Fulham.

As a player he was always the first to knock on the door to go out for a drink. But, as a manager, he was a bit dour and quiet. Don't get me wrong, we still had a laugh and a joke, but at the right time. We trained at a high tempo under his assistants, Eddie Niedzwicki and Mark Bowen.

Steve McClaren

It's good to see Steve back in English football with my old club Nottingham Forest. I think they have made a shrewd move getting him in, because it's not often you see a former England manager operating at that level.

I know he has been out of the English game for a while, but it doesn't matter. He will have made plenty of contacts during his spells in Holland and Germany and can bring some top-class foreign players to the club.

I know from past experience with him at Middlesbrough that he is a dedicated, hard worker – especially on the training ground. Alex Ferguson rated him highly at Manchester United and I know Steve will do a good job at Forest, if he is given a few bob to spend. I'm convinced of that.

Teddy Sheringham, or should I say Edward?

CHAPTER NINETEEN
The good, the bad and the ugly

I have had the pleasure of playing alongside and against a lot of different what you might call 'characters' over the years. Vinnie Jones, Paul Gascoigne, Jimmy Bullard and Robbie Savage are four that spring to mind. Peter Schmeichel was out there on his own as far as goalkeepers go.

And the list of best players I have played against would have to be topped by the likes of Eric Cantona, Ryan Giggs, Thierry Henry and Dennis Bergkamp. Like Lionel Messi (who is the best player in the best team I have ever seen) Bergkamp had the ability to make a complete mug of you. I never really feared any team, but I must admit that Blackburn, and Alan Shearer, have given me a few sleepless nights over the years.

My list of favourite Forest players would also be a long one. Stuart Pearce, Des Walker, Stan Collymore, Bryan Roy, Roy Keane, Lars Bohinen and Nigel Clough would be up there at the top.

The way Nigel held the ball up to buy a free-kick on the edge of the box was amazing and he scored 101 goals in 311 games for Forest. He was brilliant, considering he couldn't run! But he was so skilful that he didn't have to move very far, did he? Brian Clough used to refer to his son as "Our No.9" which I always found strange.

Des Walker was, for a time, probably among the best defenders in the world. It's a pity he wasted a year playing full-back in Italy. People wonder why he only scored one League goal during his career.

The fact is, he was so laid back that he couldn't be bothered to go over the half-way line. We tried to encourage him to take penalties just to get a goal against his name, but he wasn't bothered. When he used to have a good game, Brian Clough would take Des's boots off. Des was certainly a bit special. Not a bad passer, exceptionally quick and a great reader of the game. And he was a great talker. Boy could he talk; he never shut up. He had an opinion on everything and he was always right, but he was one of the best centre-halves England has ever had. He was top drawer. He's a great lad and I've got a lot of time for him. He never seems to get any older and still looks as fit as a fiddle these days.

Gareth Southgate is also one of the best defenders I have played behind while I admire Steve Stone, who started out in the youth team with me at Forest as a full-back. He did superbly well to come back after breaking his leg THREE times and catching a flesh-eating disease in hospital.

Bryan Roy was also unbelievable. He had great close skill that made it almost impossible to take the ball off him. I played against him once in an international tournament for 16-year-olds when he was with Ajax and he stood out like a sore thumb. It was a shame his career at Forest was hit by injury.

One of my heroes was the controversial former Liverpool 'keeper Bruce Grobbelaar. He was an inspirational 'keeper and I've seen him make stops that nobody else could do. His agility was fantastic and, even in his late 30s, he was capable of breathtaking saves.

I'm pleased to say I've got on well with most of them and I'm proud to call some of them friends. But there is always one exception to the rule! I fell out with Mark Bright once after he snubbed me.

It happened when Nigel Jemson and John Sheridan were at Sheffield Wednesday and they invited me up for a lads' night out. Mark Bright arrived late and went and bought everyone a drink – except me. It embarrassed me at the time, but I'm not one to hold grudges and we are OK now. In no particular order, I give you.....

Dec 26: Nottm Forest (H) Drew 0-0
Dec 29: Walsall (H) Lost 0-2
Jan 1: Leeds Utd (A) Won 3-1
Jan 12: Brighton (H) Drew 1-1
Jan 19: Yeovil (A) Drew 0-0
Jan 22: Gillingham (A) Drew 0-0
Jan 29: Carlisle (H) Won 2-0
Feb 2: Swansea (A) Lost 1-2
Feb 9: Gillingham (H) Won 2-1
Feb 12: Bristol Rovers (A) Lost 0-1
Feb 16: Yeovil (H) Won 3-0
Feb 23: Brighton (A) Lost 0-1
Feb 26: Swindon (H) Drew 2-2
Mar 1: Port Vale (A) Won 3-0
Mar 4: Hartlepool (H) Lost 0-1
Mar 8: Tranmere (H) Won 3-1
Mar 11: Bournemouth (H) Won 2-0
Mar 29: Huddersfield (H) Won 4-1
Apr 5: Swindon Town (A) Lost 0-3
Apr 12: Orient (H) Won 2-0
Apr 19: Northampton (A) Lost 0-2
Apr 26: Cheltenham (H) Won 2-1
May 3: Crewe (A) Won 4-1

2008-09 Div 1 (21 apps)
Aug 9:   Millwall (H) Won 4-3
Aug 16: Leeds Utd (A) Won 2-0
Agu 23: Cheltenham (H) Won 4-0
Aug 30: Colchester (A) Drew 2-2
Sept 6:   Tranmere (A) Won 1-0
Sept 13: MK Dons (H) Won 2-0
Sept 20: Hartlepool (A) Drew 3-3
Sept 27: Huddersfield (H) Drew 1-1
Oct 3:   Stockport (A) Lost 1-3
Oct 12: Hereford Utd (H) Won 4-0
Oct 18: Leicester City (H) Drew 1-1
Oct 21: Bristol Rovers (A) Lost 0-2
Oct 25: Swindon (A) Lost 0-2
Oct 28: Scunthorpe (H) Won 3-0
Nov 1:   Yeovil (H) Lost 0-2
Nov 15: Northampton (A) Won 1-0
Nov 22: Southend (A) Won 2-1
Nov 25: Walsall (H) Won 3-2
Dec 6:   Brighton (H) Drew 1-1
Apr 18: Brighton (A) Lost 1-3
Apr 25: Southend (H) Drew 1-1

Chesterfield
2009-10 Div 2 (4 apps)
Aug 8: Torquay (A) Lost 0-2
Dec 12: Cheltenham (H) Won 1-0
Dec 26: Lincoln (A) Lost 1-2
Jan 23: Shrewsbury (H) Lost 0-1

Printed by

Hickling&Squires

print solution

T   01773 536400
F   01773 718646
E   hi@hickling-squires.co.uk
W   www.hickling-squires.co.uk

quick kick is good, but try and avoid hitting the referee!

Mark Crossley's League career

Nottingham Forest

1988-89 Div 1 (2 apps)
Oct 26: Liverpool (H) Won 2-1
Oct 29: Newcastle (A) Won 1-0

1989-90 Div 1 (8 apps)
Nov 12: Man Utd (A) Lost 0-1
Nov 18: Man City (A) Won 3-0
Nov 25: Everton (H) Won 1-0
Dec 2: Aston Villa (A) Lost 1-2
Apr 14: Liverpool (A) Drew 2-2
Apr 16: Luton Town (H) Won 3-0
Apr 21: Southampton (A) Lost 0-2
May 2: Man Utd (H) Won 4-0

1990-91 Div 1 (38 apps)
Aug 25: QPR (H) Drew 1-1
Aug 28: Liverpool (A) Lost 0-2
Sept 1: Coventry City (A) Drew 2-2
Sept 8: Southampton (H) Won 3-1
Sept 15: Palace (A) Drew 2-2
Sept 22: Arsenal (H) Lost 0-2
Sept 29: Man Utd (A) Won 1-0
Oct 7: Everton (H) Won 3-1
Oct 20: Chelsea (A) Drew 0-0
Oct 24: Spurs (H) Lost 1-2
Nov 3: Leeds Utd (A) Lost 1-3
Nov 10: Aston Villa (A) Drew 1-1
Nov 17: Sunderland (H) Won 2-0
Nov 24: Derby County (A) Lost 1-2
Dec 1: Luton Town (H) Drew 2-2
Dec 15: QPR (A) Won 2-1
Dec 22: Sheffield Utd (A) Lost 2-3
Dec 26: Wimbledon (H) Won 2-1
Dec 31: Man City (H) Lost 1-3
Jan 2: Norwich City (A) Won 6-2
Jan 12: Coventry City (H) Won 3-0
Jan 19: Southampton (A) Drew 1-1
Feb 2: Crystal Palace (H) Lost 0-1
Feb 16: Sunderland (A) Lost 0-1
Feb 23: Aston Villa (H) Drew 2-2
Mar 2: Luton Town (A) Lost 0-1
Mar 16: Man Utd (H) Drew 1-1
Mar 20: Arsenal (A) Drew 1-1
Mar 23: Everton (A) Drew 0-0

Mar 30: Wimbledon (A) Lost 1-3
Apr 1: Sheffield Utd (H) Won 2-0
Apr 6: Manchester City (A) Lost 1-3
Apr 10: Derby County (H) Won 1-0
Apr 20: Chelsea (H) Won 7-0
Apr 24: Norwich City (H) Won 5-0
May 4: Spurs (A) Drew 1-1
May 6: Liverpool (H) Won 2-1

1991-92 Div 1 (42 apps)
Aug 17: Everton (H) Won 2-1
Aug 20: Leeds Utd (A) Lost 0-1
Aug 24: Notts County (A) Won 4-0
Aug 26: Spurs (H) Lost 1-3
Aug 31: Oldham (H) Won 3-1
Sep 4: Man City (A) Lost 1-2
Sep 7: Sheffield Wed (A) Lost 1-2
Sep 14: Wimbledon (H) Won 4-2
Sep 21: Aston Villa (A) Lost 1-3
Sep 28: West Ham Utd (H) Drew 2-2
Oct 5: QPR (A) Won 2-0
Oct 19: Sheffield Utd (A) Lost 2-4
Oct 26: Southampton (H) Lost 1-3
Nov 2: Norwich (A) Drew 0-0
Nov 16: Coventry City (H) Won 1-0
Nov 23: Crystal Palace (H) Won 5-1
Nov 30: Chelsea (A) Lost 0-1
Dec 8: Arsenal (H) Won 3-2
Dec 14: Liverpool (A) Lost 0-2
Dec 22: Leeds Utd (H) Drew 0-0
Dec 26: Spurs (A) Won 2-1
Dec 28: Oldham (A) Lost 1-2
Jan 1: Luton Town (H) Drew 1-1
Jan 11: Notts County (H) Drew 1-1
Jan 19: Everton (A) Drew 1-1
Feb 1: Sheffield Utd (H) Lost 2-5
Feb 22: Chelsea (H) Drew 1-1
Mar 3: Crystal Palace (A) Drew 0-0
Mar 11: Coventry City (A) Won 2-0
Mar 14: Norwich City (H) Won 2-0
Mar 18: Man United (H) Won 1-0
Mar 21: Man City (H) Won 2-0
Mar 31: Arsenal (A) Drew 3-3
Apr 2: Wimbledon (A) Lost 0-3
Apr 4: Sheffield Wed (H) Lost 0-2

Apr 8:   Southampton (A) Won 1-0
Apr 14: Luton Town (A) Lost 1-2
Apr 18: Aston Villa (H) Won 2-0
Apr 20: Man United (A) Won 2-1
Apr 22: Liverpool (H) Drew 1-1
Apr 25: QPR (H) Drew 1-1
May 2: West Ham Utd (A) Lost 0-3

1992-93 Premiership (37 apps)
Aug 16: Liverpool (H) Won 1-0
Aug 19: Sheffield Wed (A) Lost 0-2
Aug 22: Oldham Ath (A) Lost 3-5
Aug 28: Man Utd (H) Lost 0-2
Aug 31: Norwich City (A) Lost 1-3
Sept 5: Blackburn (A) Lost 1-4
Sept 12: Sheffield Wed (H) Lost 1-2
Sept 21: Coventry City (H) Drew 1-1
Sept 26: Chelsea (A) Drew 0-0
Oct 3:   Man City (A) Drew 2-2
Oct 17: Arsenal (H) Lost 0-1
Oct 21: Middlesbrough (H) Won 1-0
Oct 24: Sheffield Utd (A) Drew 0-0
0ct 31: Ipswich Town (H) Lost 0-1
Nov 7:   Everton (H) Lost 0-1
Nov 21: Crystal Palace (A) Drew 1-1
Nov 28: Southampton (H) Lost 1-2
Dec 5: Leeds Utd (A) Won 4-1
Dec 12: Aston Villa (A) Lost 1-2
Dec 20: Wimbledon (H) Drew 1-1
Dec 28: Spurs (A) Lost 1-2
Jan 9: Coventry City (A) Won 1-0
Jan 16: Chelsea (H) Won 3-0
Jan 27: Man United (A) Lost 0-2
Jan 30: Oldham (H) Won 2-0
Feb 6: Liverpool (A) Drew 0-0
Feb 20: Middlesbrough (A) Won 2-1
Feb 24: QPR (H) Won 1-0
Feb 27: Manchester City (H) Lost 0-2
Mar 3: Crystal Palace (H) Drew 1-1
Mar 13: Everton (A) Lost 0-3
Mar 17: Norwich City (H) Lost 0-3
Mar 21: Leeds Utd (H) Drew 1-1
Mar 24: Southampton (A) Won 2-1
Apr 4: Aston Villa (H) Lost 0-1
Apr 7: Blackburn (H) Lost 1-3
Apr 10: QPR (A) Lost 3-4

1993-94 Div 1 (36 apps)
Aug 15: Southend (A) Drew 1-1
Aug 18: Derby County (H) Drew 1-1
Aug 21: Grimsby Town (H) Won 5-3
Aug 24: Crystal Palace (A) Lost 0-2
Aug 28: Luton Town (A) Won 2-1
Sep 11: Barnsley (A) Lost 0-1
Sep 19: Stoke City (H) Lost 2-3
Sep 26: Bolton (A) Lost 3-4
Oct 2:   Portsmouth (A) Drew 1-1
Oct 16: Tranmere Rovers (H) Won 2-1
Oct 20: Oxford Utd (H) Drew 0-0
Oct 24: Leicester City (A) Lost 0-1
Oct 30: Notts County (H) Won 1-0
Nov 3:   Millwall (H) Lost 1-3
Nov 6:   Birmingham (A) Won 3-0
Nov 10: Wolves (A) Drew 1-1
Nov 21: West Brom (A) Won 2-0
Nov 27: Sunderland (A) Won 3-2
Dec 4: Birmingham City (A) Won 1-0
Dec 19: Southend Utd (H) Won 2-0
Dec 27: Middlesbrough (H) Drew 1-1
Dec 28: Bristol City (A) Won 4-1
Jan 1: Charlton (H) Drew 1-1
Jan 3: Watford (A) Won 2-1
Jan 16: Tranmere Rovers (A) Won 2-1
Jan 23: Wolves (H) Drew 0-0
Feb 6: Leicester City (H) Won 4-0
Feb 12: Notts County (A) Lost 1-2
Feb 19: Crystal Palace (H) Drew 1-1
Feb 26: Oxford Utd (A) Lost 0-1
Mar 2: Peterborough (H) Won 2-0
Mar 5: Luton Town (H) Won 2-0
Mar 12: Stoke City (A) Won 1-0
Mar 16: Barnsley (H) Won 2-1
Mar 19: Bolton (H) Won 3-2
Mar 26: Portsmouth (A) Lost 1-2
Mar 30: Watford (H) Won 2-1
Apr 2: Middlesbrough (A) Drew 2-2
Apr 4: Bristol City (H) Drew 0-0
Apr 9: Charlton (A) Won 1-0
Apr 17: Millwall (A) Drew 2-2
Apr 24: West Brom (H) Won 2-1
Apr 27: Derby County (H) Won 2-0
Apr 30: Peterborough (A) Won 3-2
May 3: Grimsby Town (A) Drew 0-0
May 8: Sunderland (H) Drew 2-2

1994-95 Premiership (42 apps)
Aug 20: Ipswich Town (A) Won 1-0
Aug 22: Manchester Utd (H) Drew 1-1
Aug 27: Leicester City (H) Won 1-0
Aug 30: Everton (A) Won 2-1
Sept 10: Sheffield Wed (H) Won 4-1
Sept 17: Southampton (A) Drew 1-1
Sept 24: Spurs (A) Won 4-1
Oct 2: QPR (H) Won 3-2
Oct 8: Man City (A) Drew 3-3
Oct 17: Wimbledon (H) Won 3-1
Oct 22: Aston Villa (A) Won 2-0
Oct 29: Blackburn (H) Lost 0-2
Nov 5: Liverpool (A) Lost 0-1
Nov 7: Newcastle (H) Drew 0-0
Nov 19: Chelsea (H) Lost 0-1
Nov 26: Leeds Utd (A) Lost 0-1
Dec 3: Arsenal (A) Drew 2-2
Dec 10: Ipswich (H) Won 4-1
Dec 17: Man Utd (A) Won 2-1
Dec 26: Coventry (A) Drew 0-0
Dec 27: Norwich (H) Won 1-0
Dec 31: West Ham (A) Lost 1-3
Jan 2: Crystal Palace (H) Won 1-0
Jan 14: Blackburn (A) Lost 0-3
Jan 21: Aston Villa (H) Lost 1-2
Jan 25: Chelsea (A) Won 2-0
Feb 4: Liverpool (H) Drew 1-1
Feb 11: Newcastle (A) Lost 1-2
Feb 21: Arsenal (A) Lost 0-1
Feb 26: QPR (A) Drew 1-1
Mar 4: Spurs (H) Drew 2-2
Mar 8: Everton (H) Won 2-1
Mar 11: Leicester City (A) Won 4-2
Mar 18: Southampton (H) Won 3-0
Mar 22: Leeds (H) Won 3-0
Apr 1: Sheffield Wed (A) Won 7-1
Apr 8: West Ham (H) Drew 1-1
Apr 12: Norwich (A) Won 1-0
Apr 17: Coventry (H) Won 2-0
Apr 29: Crystal Palace (A) Won 2-1
May 6: Man City (H) Won 1-0
May 13: Wimbledon (A) Drew 2-2

1995-96 Premiership (38 apps)
Aug 19: Southampton (A) Won 4-3
Aug 23: Chelsea (H) Drew 0-0
Aug 26: West Ham (H) Drew 1-1
Aug 29: Arsenal (A) Drew 1-1
Sept 9: Coventry (A) Drew 1-1
Sept 17: Everton (H) Won 3-2
Sept 23: Aston Villa (A) Drew 1-1
Sept 30: Man City (H) Won 3-0
Oct 14: Spurs (A) Won 1-0
Oct 21: Bolton (H) Won 3-2
Oct 28: QPR (A) Drew 1-1
Nov 6: Wimbeldon (H) Won 4-1
Nov 18: Blackburn (A) Lost 0-7
Nov 27: Man Utd (H) Drew 1-1
Dec 2: Bolton (A) Drew 1-1
Dec 10: Aston Villa (H) Drew 1-1
Dec 18: Man City (A) Drew 1-1
Dec 23: Newcastle Utd (A) Lost 1-3
Dec 26: Sheffield Wed (H) Won 1-0
Dec 30: Middlesbrough (H) Won 1-0
Jan 1: Liverpool (A) Lost 2-4
Jan 13: Southampton (H) Won 1-0
Jan 20: Chelsea (A) Lost 0-1
Jan 31: Leeds (H) Won 2-1
Feb 3: West Ham (A) Lost 0-1
Feb 10: Arsenal (H) Lost 0-1
Feb 24: Everton (A) Lost 0-3
Mar 2: Sheffield Wed (A) Won 3-1
Mar 16: Middlesbrough (A) Drew 1-1
Mar 23: Liverpool (H) won 1-0
Mar 30: Wimbledon (A) Lost 0-1
Apr 6: Spurs (H) Won 2-1
Apr 8: Leeds (A) Won 3-1
Apr 13: Blackburn (H) Lost 1-5
Apr 17: Coventry (H) Drew 0-0
Apr 28: Man Utd (A) Lost 0-5
May 2: Newacstle Utd (H) Drew 1-1
May 5: QPR (H) Won 3-0

1996-97 Premiership (34 apps)
Aug 17: Coventry (A) Won 3-0
Aug 21: Sunderland (H) Lost 1-4
Aug 24: Middlesbrough (H) Drew 1-1
Sept 4: Southampton (A) Drew 2-2
Sept 7: Leicester City (H) Drew 0-0
Sept 14: Man Utd (A) Lost 1-4
Sept 21: West Ham (H) Lost 0-2
Sept 28: Chelsea (A) Drew 1-1
Oct 12: Leeds Utd (A) Lost 0-2

Oct 19: Derby County (H) Drew 1-1
Oct 28: Everton (H) Lost 0-1
Nov 2: Aston Villa (A) Lost 0-2
Nov 18: Sheffield Wed (A) Lost 0-2
Nov 25: Blackburn (H) Drew 2-2
Nov 30: Wimbledon (A) Lost 0-1
Dec 9: Newcastle Utd (H) Drew 0-0
Dec 17: Liverpool (A) Lost 2-4
Dec 21: Arsenal (H) Won 2-1
Dec 26: Man Utd (H) Lost 0-4
Dec 28: Leicester (A) Drew 2-2
Jan 1: West Ham (A) Won 1-0
Jan 11: Chelsea (H) Won 2-0
Jan 19: Spurs (H) Won 2-1
Jan 29: Coventry (H) Lost 0-1
Feb 1: Everton (A) Lost 0-2
Feb 22: Aston Villa (H) Drew 0-0
Mar 1: Spurs (A) Won 1-0
Mar 5: Sheffield Wed (H) Lost 0-3
Mar 8: Arsenal (A) Lost 0-2
Mar 11: Blackburn (A) Drew 1-1
Mar 15: Liverpool (H) Drew 1-1
Mar 22: Sunderland (A) Drew 1-1
Mar 24: Middlesbrough (A) Drew 1-1
Apr: 5: Southampton (H) Lost 1-3

Millwall
1997-98 Div 2 (13 apps)
Feb 21: Northampton (H) Drew 0-0
Feb 25: Watford (H) Drew 1-1
Feb 28: Oldham (A) Drew 1-1
Mar 3: Carlisle (A) Lost 0-1
Mar 7: Gillingham (H) Won 1-0
Mar 14: Fulham (A) Won 2-1
Mar 17: Wrexham (A) Lost 0-1
Mar 21: Burnley (H) Won 1-0
Mar 25: Preston (A) Lost 0-1
Mar 28: Chesterfield (A) Lost 1-3
Apr 4:Bristol Rovers (H) Drew 1-1
Apr 11: Walsall (A) Lost 0-2
Apr 13: Plymouth (H) Drew 1-1

Nottingham Forest
1998-99 Premiership (12 apps)
Feb 27: Charlton (A) Drew 0-0
Mar 10: Newcastle (H) Lost 1-2

Mar 13: Wimbeldon (A) Won 3-1
Mar 20: Middlesbrough (H) Lost 1-2
Apr 3: Leeds (A) Lost 1-3
Apr 5: Liverpool (H) Drew 2-2
Apr 10: Derby County (A) Lost 0-1
Apr 17: Spurs (H) Lost 0-1
Apr 24: Aston Villa (A) Lost 0-2
May 1: Sheffield Wed (H) Won 2-0
May 8: Blackburn (A) Won 2-1
May 16: Leicester (H) Won 1-0

1999-00 Div 1 (20 apps)
Aug 7: Ipswich (A) Lost 1-3
Aug 14: Grimsby (H) Won 2-0
Aug 20: WBA (A) Drew 2-2
Aug 28: QPR (H) Drew 1-1
Aug 30: Man City (A) Lost 0-1
Sep 11: Swindon (A) Drew 0-0
Sep 19: Wolves (H) Drew 1-1
Oct 1: Barnsley (H) Won 3-0
Oct 16: Sheff Utd (A) Lost 1-2
Oct 19: Port Vale (A) Won 2-0
Oct 23: Stockport (H) Won 2-0
Oct 27: Bolton (H) Drew 1-1
Oct 30: Barnsley (A) Lost 0-1
Nov 6: Norwich (A) Lost 0-1
Nov 14: Huddersfield (H) Lost 1-3
Nov 20: Tranmere (A) Lost 0-3
Nov 24: Portsmouth (H) Won 2-0
Nov 27: Crystal Palace (A) Lost 0-2
Jan 15: Grimsby (A) Lost 3-4
Jan 29: QPR (A) Lost 1-2

Middlesbrough
2000-01 Premier (4 apps + 1 sub*)
Sep 30: Southampton (A) Won 3-1*
Oct 16: Newcastle Utd (H) Lost 1-3
Oct 21: Charlton (A) Lost 0-1
Oct 28: Ipswich (A) Lost 1-2
Nov 4: Arsenal (H) Lost 0-1

2001-02 (17 apps + 1 sub*)
Sep 8: Newcaastle (H) Lost 1-4*
Sep 23: Chelsea (A) Drew 2-2
Oct 13: Charlton (A) Drew 0-0
Nov 17: Aston Villa (A) Drew 0-0

Nov 25: Ipswich (H) Drew 0-0
Dec 1: Blackburn (A) Won 1-0
Dec 8: Liverpool (A) Lost 0-2
Dec 15: Man Utd (H) Lost 0-1
Dec 26: Newcastle (A) Lost 0-3
Dec 29: Arsenal (A) Lost 1-2
Jan 1: Everton (H) Won 1-0
Jan 12: Fulham (A) Lost 1-2
Jan 19: Bolton (H) Drew 1-1
Jan 29: Sunderland (A) Won 1-0
Feb 3: Charlton (H) Drew 0-0
Feb 9: Leeds (H) Drew 2-2
Mar 30: Spurs (H) Drew 1-1
Apr 1: Derby County (A) Won 1-0

Stoke City

2002-03 Div 1 (12 apps)
Nov 30: Gillingham (A) Drew 1-1
Mar 8: Ipswich (A) Drew 0-0
Mar 15: Sheffield Utd (H) Drew 0-0
Mar 18: Wolves (A) Drew 0-0
Mar 22: Watford (A) Won 2-1
Apr 5: Gillingham (H) Drew 0-0
Apr 9: Rotherham (H) Won 2-0
Apr 12: Millwall (A) Lost 1-3
Apr 19: Wimbledon (H) Won 2-1
Apr 21: Coventry (A) Won 1-0
Apr 26: Crystal Palace (A) Lost 0-1
May 4: Reading (H) Won 1-0

Fulham

2003-04 Premiership (1 app)
Nov 2: Liverpool (H) Lost 1-2

2004-05 (5 apps + 1 sub*)
Oct 30: Spurs (H) Won 2-0
Nov 7: Newcastle Utd (A) Won 4-1
Nov 13: Chelsea (H) Lost 1-4
Nov 20: Everton (A) Lost 0-1
Nov 27: Blackburn (H) Lost 0-2
May 4: Newcastle Utd (H) Lost 1-3*

2005-06 (13 apps)
Oct 1: Manchester Utd (H) Lost 2-3
Oct 17: Charlton Ath (A) Drew 1-1
Oct 22: Liverpool (H) Won 2-0

Nov 27: Bolton (H) Won 2-1
Dec 3: WBA (A) Drew 0-0
Dec 10: Birmingham (A) Lost 0-1
Dec 17: Blackburn (H) Won 2-1
Dec 26: Chelsea (A) Lost 2-3
Dec 28: Aston Villa (H) Drew 3-3
Mar 19: Chelsea (H) Won 1-0
Mar 25: Aston VIlla (A) Drew 0-0
Apr 1: Portsmouth (H) Lost 1-3

Sheffield Wednesday

2006-07 Championship (17 apps)
Nov 11: Ipswich Town (A) Won 2-0
Nov 18: Coventry (A) Lost 1-3
Nov 25: Cardiff (H) Drew 0-0
Nov 28: WBA (H) Won 3-1
Dec 2: Leicester City (A) Won 4-1
Dec 9: Norwich (A) Won 2-1
Dec 16: Birmingham (H) Lost 0-3
Dec 23: Southampton (H) Drew 3-3
Dec 26: Stoke City (A) Won 2-1
Dec 30: Barnsley (A) Won 3-0
Jan 1: Hull City (H) Lost 1-2
Jan 13: Derby County (A) Lost 0-1
Jan 20: Sunderland (H) Lost 2-4
Jan 31: Southampton (A) Lost 1-2
Feb 3: Preston (H) Lost 1-3
Feb 10: Burnley (A) Drew 1-1
Feb 20: Luton Town (A) Lost 2-3

Oldham

2007-08 Div 1 (38 apps)
Aug 11: Swansea (H) Won 2-1
Aug 18: Carlisle (A) Lost 0-1
Aug 25: Bristol Rovers (H) Lost 0-1
Sept 1: Hartlepool (A) Lost 1-4
Sept 15: Southend (H) Lost 0-1
Sept 22: Walsall (A) Won 3-0
Sept 29: Crewe (H) Won 3-2
Oct 2: Leeds United (H) Lost 0-1
Oct 6: Cheltenham (A) Drew 1-1
Nov 17: Port Vale (H) Drew 1-1
Nov 24: Bournemouth (A) Won 3-0
Dec 4: Luton Town (H) Drew 1-1
Dec 8: Doncaster (H) Drew 1-1
Dec 15: Millwall (H) Won 3-2
Dec 22: Southend (A) Won 1-0